LONDON
through the Ages

LONDON
through the Ages

The Story of a City and its Citizens
54 B.C.—A.D. 1944

by

DOROTHY MARGARET STUART

With illustrations from original
sources by Sheila Maguire

NEW YORK

E. P. DUTTON & CO., INC.

Library of Congress Catalog Card Number: 58–6787

FOR

DENNY

WHO LOVES OLD LONDON
AS MUCH AS I DO

Foreword

THE long chronicle of London is so packed with incident and so rich in colour, and it touches at so many points the history not only of Great Britain but of the world, that no single book could possibly trace its course in full. I have therefore tried to paint the City as a many-hued backcloth and to set the Londoners as living and moving actors in the centre of the scene. My readers will meet many famous folk, but they will also see the constantly-changing pageant in the streets, the daily lives of merchants and craftsmen and their families, the playhouses and the pleasure-gardens, and there are dark patches, too, to throw into brighter relief the other parts of the picture. `

The story of London is the story of her citizens. They have altered very little in a thousand years; and while they remain the same witty, imperturbable and indomitable people, the heart of England will never miss a beat.

D.M.S.

Contents

Frontispiece: The Tower of London in the XV Century, with Charles of Orleans looking out of the window, Old London Bridge and the City in the distance.

From an Illuminated Manuscript in the British Museum

Acknowledgements

The seven illustrations on pages 213, 217, 219, 224, 225, 227 and 229 are reproduced by courtesy of the proprietors of *Punch*.

The drawing of the Temple of Mithras on page 7 is reproduced by courtesy of the *Daily Telegraph*.

CHAPTER I

Lonely Estuary to Walled Town

'THE Britons', wrote Julius Caesar, 'call a thick wood enclosed with a rampart and a ditch a "town"'; but when that remarkable man marched with his Roman Legions up the Thames valley in the year 54 B.C. it is doubtful whether he found either rampart or ditch where London stands to-day. If there was anything in the nature of a settlement it would be a small huddle of turf and wicker huts on what is now the Surrey shore—a perfect spot, beside a broad estuary, much broader then than now and much shallower, teeming with fish and fowl, and sheltered by forests where the red deer roved.

A Celtic tribe called the Trinovantes occupied this region; to the north were the dwellings of their neighbours, the Catuvellani. These tribes were not barbarians, even though by Roman standards they may have been a simple and uncouth folk. They were skilful weavers, potters and goldsmiths: they traded with their Gaulish kinsmen in what is now northern France, exporting hunting hounds and hides, amber and corn; swords and javelins of well-tempered bronze were their weapons in war, and they drove low chariots drawn by a fleet and hardy breed of horses.

When word came to them that Gaul had been invaded and conquered by a terrible Roman general called Julius Caesar the men of southern Britain did not hesitate to send such aid as they could to help their fellow-Celts across the Channel. It was to teach them to meddle no more in Gaulish

affairs that Caesar made his two famous landings, first in
55 B.C. and then a year later. On his second visit he crossed
the river Thames 'at the single spot where it is fordable on
foot'.[1] Learned men still argue quite fiercely as to where that
spot then was; some favour Brentford, others recall that
Chelsea was the highest point reached by the tide and that
skulls, of both the Roman and the British type, have been
found there in the river bed, together with shields, helmets and
spears which may well be the relics of a desperate battle.
One thing at least is certain. The river already bore a name
very similar to what it bears to-day. Every time that a
modern Londoner speaks of 'the Thames' he is uttering a
word which would be understood by the long-vanished
people who paddled their canoes and cast their nets in its
waters two thousand years ago.

As London did not yet exist the rest of the story is not
really hers, though it was the Trinovantes, the tribe dwelling
round the Thames estuary, who surprised Julius Caesar by
offering to submit to him. With the waning of the year that
great general wisely decided to withdraw across the Channel.
Not for more than ninety years would Roman words of
command be heard in the Thames Valley.

In the year 43 of the Christian era the Romans returned,
this time for a stay of more than three centuries. After an
able general called Aulus Plautius had directed the actual
fighting to a more or less victorious conclusion, Claudius
Caesar, a good-humoured, rather quaint and clumsy Emperor, great-grand-nephew of the 'mightiest Julius', paid a
brief visit to this newest province of that Roman Empire
which had sprawled over the greater part of Europe and was
overflowing into Africa and Asia Minor. Not even his golden
breast-plate and his escort of elephants could make him an

---

[1] Caesar's own words, in his account of the expedition. He does not mention an
elephant but an early tradition says that he had one with him.

impressive figure: but his coming marked a new stage in the history of Britain—and of London.

The red deer and the wild duck, the otter and the heron had the northern bank of the Thames estuary to themselves no longer. Low huts, built of turf and thatched with wicker, had begun to cluster there in sufficient numbers to form a settlement, and presently the settlement was important enough to be dignified by a name—Londinium. It has been suggested that this name came from two Celtic words meaning a stream and a stronghold; but modern scholarship prefers the theory that some local Celtic chieftain was com-memorated in the little township on the high ground later known as 'Cornhill'.

The conquest of Britain was completed in the year 86 by the wise and warlike Agricola. His son-in-law, Tacitus, writing the story of his great achievements, makes the first recorded allusion to Londinium, 'exceedingly famous' he wrote, 'as a centre of commerce, crowded with merchants'.

As was their wont, the Romans had set about building a new town worthy of the name. The site was well chosen; and so rapidly did the work proceed that the tile-makers and the brick-makers had difficulty in keeping pace. The merchants mentioned by Tacitus had a fine covered Forum or market-place in which to meet and transact business; local government was directed from the equally handsome Basilica. Prosperous inhabitants, British and Roman, lived in delightful villas with gaily-painted walls, floors inlaid with mosaic in elaborate designs, and an efficient central-heating system.

Pillared temples were dedicated impartially to a variety of gods, native and imported. So long as the local cult did not conflict with the state religion of Caesar-worship the Romans were the most tolerant of rulers. They were inci-dentally the best town-planners in history. Londinium was a typical example of their skill. The interests of the merchants were carefully considered. There were long wharves where trading galleys could tie up. A bridge, supported on wooden piles, spanned the river at a point eastward of the future medieval bridge and even further east than the existing one.

Gladiator's Tomb with inscription in Greek

During his active career he may have been one of the most popular figures in Londinium

In the Guildhall Museum

There was a circus on the southern bank for gladiatorial and wild beast shows; there was a track for chariot-racing; there were public baths, hot and cold. Small coins still dredged from the mud beneath the site of the wooden bridge are believed to have been offerings made to the god of the river.

Many relics of Roman-British life are brought to light every year: a lady's jet hair pin, a child's bronze toy, a patch of inlaid pavement, a chip of glossy red pottery. At a certain level traces of fire are found, melted coins, charred wood, heat-cracked tiles. These are reminders of the war waged by Boadicea, Queen of the tribe of the Iceni, against Rome, to avenge the wrongs inflicted upon her and her people by a comparatively small number of grasping and unscrupulous Roman officials.

When the Iceni surged southward the Governor of Britain, Suetonius Paulinus, was far away in the west on an expedition against the Druids of Mona (Anglesey); but he turned hastily and marched to meet this unexpected danger. Londinium, being unfortified, could not be defended; he decided to evacuate the city, intending to gather fresh forces and call together more Legions while the Iceni plundered and spoiled. He did offer however to take with him any Londoners able and willing to come. Some of them preferred to remain in their homes, either because they lacked the strength to keep up with the well-known rapid march of the soldiery or, as the Roman historian suggests, because 'they loved the place so dearly that they could not bear to leave'. They may even have hoped that Boadicea, being a woman, and a woman of their own blood, might deal mercifully with them.

There was no mercy in the heart of the 'British warrior-Queen'. Londinium, with all its proud temples and public buildings and painted villas, was burned to ashes and such of its inhabitants as did not perish in the fire were massacred by the exulting Iceni. But against the might of Rome one small British tribe, however warlike, could not prevail. Soon the columns and the arches rose again; craft from all parts of the Roman Empire crowded the port of Londinium, and wagons laden with merchandise creaked and lurched through the streets—the gauge of the wagon-wheels being almost exactly the same as that of a modern British Railway train.

At the height of its splendour Roman London covered a larger area than any other city in Roman Britain—between 325 and 350 acres, some five miles in circumference. The Basilica, situated where Leadenhall Market now stands, was only fifty feet less in length than St. Paul's Cathedral, and it was supported by columns forty feet high. Not far from where the Lord Mayor lives to-day was the official residence of the Governor, complete with hot and cold baths and central heating.

An ancient Roman law forbade the burial of the dead—even of their ashes—within the city walls. That is why so many tombs are unearthed upon what were then the outskirts. The widow of a gladiator set up a memorial to him with an inscription in Greek: but it is usually in Latin that we read of 'loving wives', 'matchless husbands', and 'dutiful children'.

Among the many gods and goddesses worshipped in Londinium was the Persian sun-god Mithras, whose cult was especially popular with merchants and soldiers. In the autumn of 1954 thousands of modern Londoners queued up to see the ruins of a Mithraic temple unearthed at Walbrook and dating from the second century A.D. Such temples were usually built underground, and the sacrifices and ceremonies of the sun-god were performed by torchlight. The central object would be an image of Mithras in the act of slaying a bull. On either side were statues representing night and day, and other gods were occasionally admitted, the Egyptian Serapis, for example, whose bearded head was discovered beneath the Walbrook Mithraeum, with various fragments of sculpture. It seems probable that these idols were hastily buried some time in the fourth century to preserve them from destruction at the hands of the Christians.

Mithraism was a man's religion. No goddess was honoured and no woman might take part in the ceremonies, but the women of Londinium enjoyed a wide choice of divinities, among them Bona Fortuna, who was somehow associated with the river Thames.

The Temple of Mithras reconstructed

He was the favourite god of merchants and soldiers

By permission of the 'Daily Telegraph'

Then as now the London workman liked his little joke. Not far from the Mithraeum was discovered a tile[1] upon which some wag had scratched the words, 'Australis has

[1] In the Guildhall Museum.

been going off by himself every day for these nineteen days'.

There has quite recently been discovered and deciphered part of a letter[1] written during the first century A.D. by a British employer to the person in charge of his household in 'Londinio'. The six lines composing it were scratched with a metal pen or *stylus* on a wax tablet, and they were scratched so vigorously that they penetrated to the wooden surface behind the wax. Rufus, son of Callisumus, greets Epellicus, asks him to send a certain list, if he has made it, charges him to look carefully after everything, and instructs him to 'turn the slave-girl into cash'.

Londinium, not being a garrison city, did not enter much into the curious game of Caesar-making which spread over the Empire after the descendants of Julius Caesar died out in the half-crazy person of Nero. Later Emperors still called themselves 'Caesar', but they had no hereditary claim to the imperial purple, being chosen and acclaimed by the Army. Presently various Legions in various places began to choose Caesars of their own—there were as many as five Emperors minting their own coinage at one period—with the result that, for lack of a strong central authority, the defence of the Empire against barbarian invaders was difficult—if not impossible—to organize. Savage tribes from central and eastern Europe poured into the rich plains of Italy, Scots and Picts invaded Britain from the north, Saxon pirates poured upon the coasts of Britain and Gaul; the first shadow of the Dark Ages was creeping over Europe.

From 287 to 293 Britain had a Caesar of her own, Carausius, a curly-haired sea-pilot from the land now called Belgium. He came with a large band of followers, and caused himself to be proclaimed Emperor. He minted gold and silver coins bearing his head, he began to build a navy; then he was murdered by another would-be Caesar, a certain

[1] In the British Museum.

Allectus, whose reign was even more brief. The great war-galley discovered in 1910 in deep mud at the southern end of Westminster Bridge was probably a unit in the fleet of one or other of these upstart Caesars. She must have been a lovely craft when gilded dolphins curved round her prow and her upper-deck was shaded by an awning woven in gay colours. So perfectly fitted are the joints that no caulking[1] had been necessary.

Coin of Carausius, sea-pilot and 'Caesar'

Proclaimed in Londinium, but not destined to rule there long

British Museum

It happened that one of the associate Emperors far away in Italy was a man of strong character. His name was Flavius Constantius Chlorus, and in the year 292 he landed in Britain, defeated Allectus and his gang of toughs, entered Londinium in triumph, and was joyfully welcomed by the Londoners. In honour of this event a gold medal was struck, and here it is that London comes into the picture again. Through a turreted gate rides Constantius, spear in hand; to greet him kneels a woman with arms upraised. The monosyllable LON shows that she personifies the City. In the foreground a galley is anchored. And the inscription proudly proclaims, *Redditor lucis æternæ*—the return of light everlasting.

[1] To 'caulk 'a vessel is to twist or squeeze strands of rope or oakum between the planks.

While the light lasted—which was not for very long—
Constantius took energetic measures for the defence of a
Britain, threatened by blue-painted Picts as well as by red-
haired Saxon pirates. It was his son, Constantine the Great,
who by making Christianity the official religion of the
Roman Empire changed the whole course of history; and

*London welcomes her deliverer, Flavius
Constantius Chlorus*

Golden medal struck in honour of the occasion. A war-galley at anchor in
the foreground

                              In the Museum of Arras

it was in the reign of Constantine the Great that London
received the proud title of *Londinium Augusta*, London the
August.

The new religion spread slowly in Londinium, where the
old gods, Roman, Celtic and Asiatic, continued to be worshipped more or less faithfully. It is true that there was a
Bishop of London present at the great Church Council held
at Arles in 314; but only eleven years earlier a Roman

soldier, Albanus by name, was beheaded within twenty
miles of the City for befriending a fugitive Christian priest
from Wales.

What did they talk about, the merchants and officials, the
gladiators, the charioteers, the craftsmen, of the many-
coloured, bustling City? Trade, sport, the day-to-day affairs
of a great mixed community? No doubt. But even the
most unthinking among them must have been troubled when
the centre of the Empire was transferred from the Tiber to
the Bosphorus, from Rome to the new, gorgeous city of
Constantinople.[1] The Tiber was remote enough, in all conscience, but the Bosphorus was more remote still. If Britain
were to be over-run by the barbarians, would help come in
time—and in sufficient force?

Round about the year 367 the Emperor Valentinian I,
being then in Gaul, sent trusted commanders to report upon
the position in south-eastern Britain. So grave was the
account they brought back, he next despatched one of his
best generals, the Spanish-born Theodosius, to restore order
and subdue the invading barbarians. Then once again the
people of Londinium Augusta, leaping for joy, hailed a
Roman victor. With him in his triumphal entry he brought
thousands of country folk whom he had rescued from the
slave-gangs of the invaders.

Meanwhile there had been a hasty strengthening of the
wall which had already for more than two hundred years
surrounded the city. It was done, says one historian, 'at
panic speed', as some of the existing fragments show. Even
broken pieces of tombstones were wedged into the gaps,
telling a silent story of desperation and dismay. It was all
in vain. The barbarians under Alaric the Goth captured and
sacked Rome in the year 410 and after 411 the tramp of
Roman military boots was heard in Londinium no more.

[1] Now called by its Turkish name of Istanbul.

The Legions were being hurriedly recalled from the outposts of the crumbling Empire.

Deserted thus by their masters, the Britons did not at once lose hope. For more than thirty years they continued to send desperate appeals to whatever far-off Caesar was uneasily, or sometimes unworthily, wearing the imperial purple. But the Romanized Britons were incapable of organizing any sort of military resistance to the foes who came pouring over them in an ever-rising flood.

When in the middle years of the fifth century Attila the Hun created an Empire extending from the banks of the Rhine to the frontiers of China, the Angles, Saxons, Jutes, Frisians and other blond, braceleted warriors became decidedly uneasy. To avoid these terrible Huns the simplest plan was clearly to invade and occupy the fertile and feebly-defended lands of southern and south-eastern Britain; and this they did with so much success that the Roman-British populations were engulfed and almost blotted out.

These newcomers cared nothing for cities. When they had taken such plunder as they cared to take, they spread out over the countryside, and settled down to the sort of life they liked, farming, hunting, and occasionally fighting.

Londinium Augusta fell into ruin and decay. Grass sprouted between the paving-stones, roofs crashed on to tessellated pavements, owls roosted in the Forum and bats swooped to and fro in the Basilica. As to the citizens there is a certain mystery, but some sort of comfortless, precarious life may still have been led within the broken walls.

Presently the city appears again on the page of history— this time under a new name. The Picts and the Caledonians were pushing southward from their hungry homelands, and towards the middle of this tumultuous fifth century Vortigern, King of Kent, invited the two Saxon brother-warriors, Hengist and Horsa, to come and help him to defend his

kingdom from these northern hordes. The story of that
foolish invitation and all the woes that followed from it
belongs to the story of England in general; but when Hengist
had defeated his former British 'friends' at Crayford we are
told that the people of Kent fled in terror and sought refuge
in 'Lundenbyrig'—that is to say, London Town. It may be

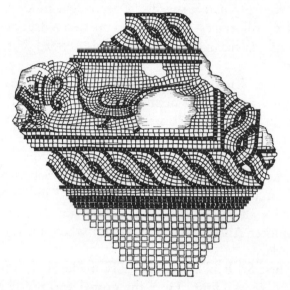

Tessellated pavement from a house in Londinium

Many such pavements lie deep beneath the modern city

that they thought they would find some supernatural protection in ruins so impressive round which so many legends
must still have clung.

Although neither the unhappy Britons nor the vigorous
Saxons dreamed yet that it was so, a force was at work which
would in the end restore civilization not only to 'Lundenbyrig' but to all the Western World. When that time came,
the city would be a unit not in a material Empire but in a
spiritual commonwealth called 'Christendom'. And towards

the end of the sixth century Pope Gregory the Great sent
his friend Augustine and a small company of monks to con-
vert the heathen Anglo-Saxons of Kent. These rough
fellows were not all Angles, or even Saxons, but it was the
Angles who gave to the island of Britain its name of 'Angle-
land' or 'England,' and it was the Saxons who imposed upon
it their vigorous native speech. Deep below modern London
there are still traces of their occupation—drinking-horns,
combs of walrus ivory, amber beads, sword hilts garnet-
studded.

Ethelbert, King of Kent, listened to the preaching of
Augustine: so did his nephew, Sebert, King of the East
Saxons, in whose kingdom London stood. The two Kings
co-operated to build a church dedicated to St. Paul on the
top of a little hill named after a legendary local personage
called Lud. Ethelbert provided the money; Sebert consented
to the use of the site. The West-Saxon King was himself
planning a church of his own, further up the river, where
Westminster Abbey now stands, and where his tomb is still
to be seen.

The first St. Paul's was probably made of wood—a small
and humble building. Here the gospel was preached by St.
Augustine's friend and fellow-missionary, Mellitus, first
Bishop of London, and it seemed as if the Christian faith had
struck root where first Celtic, and then Roman, and then
Saxon deities had been honoured. It was not so. Ethelbert's
son, Edbald, lapsed back into the old pagan creed, and
Mellitus had no choice but to return to Gaul. Though
Edbald repented later, and called him back to fill the chair
of St. Augustine as Archbishop of Canterbury, it is unlikely
that the people of London ever saw their gentle, gouty
Bishop limping to and fro among them again.

During the fifty years that elapsed before the Anglo-
Saxon Erkenwald became London's Bishop the number of

the inhabitants had increased and their ideas had altered. The former farmer-folk were learning to live and work in a walled town; they had come to realize the importance of commerce. Far away in his monastery beside the broad river Tyne the Venerable Bede heard of London as the 'mart of many nations'.

St. Augustine on his throne

Mellitus, Bishop of London, was his friend and follower

From an illuminated Manuscript

Before the seventh century closed, most of the East Saxons were Christians again. Bishop Erkenwald toiled valiantly to win the unconverted, especially the rough folk dwelling in the wild woodlands to the north of London. It was said that on a certain day when he was on his way to preach to these foresters one of the two wheels of his little wagon fell off but the other wheel continued to revolve in a miraculous manner; the wagon did not overturn, and the Saint reached his destination safely.

An even more curious legend clings round the events

following his death, which took place at the Abbey of Barking, where his sister, Ethelburga, ruled as Abbess. Mindful of the words of Holy Scripture that 'there is much virtue in the bones of a prophet', religious communities were always eager to add to their collection of relics. The monks of Chertsey, the clergy of St. Paul's, and the nuns of Barking were all equally anxious that Erkenwald should be entombed in their midst. When the clergy reached Barking ahead of the monks and started for London with the Bishop's body loud cries ascended both from the monks and the nuns, and the river Lea rose in a flood, barring the way. What happened next is well related in an old history of London.

A pious man present however exhorted the monks to peace and begged them to leave the matter to heavenly decision. The clergy of St. Paul's then broke forth into a litany. The Lea at once subsided, the sun cast down its benediction, and the clergy passed on to St. Paul's with their holy spoil.

Early in the fourteenth century a new and glorious shrine was made for St. Erkenwald, upon which three London goldsmiths were kept busy for a whole year.

Towards the end of the eighth century Anglo-Saxon Christians kneeling in St. Paul's uttered fervent 'Amens' to a new prayer which had been inserted in the Litany— 'deliver us, O Lord, from the fury of the Norsemen!' These Norsemen were the heathen Vikings from the Scandinavian peninsula, and they were beginning to make fierce swoops upon Gaul, Ireland, Scotland and Britain. They were particularly interested in monasteries and churches because of the treasures they contained: but no spoils came amiss, and their long ships with golden dragons at the prow and coloured shields slung along the sides came to be dreaded as much in Anglo-Saxon England as the ships of the Anglo-Saxons themselves had been dreaded in Roman Britain.

London suffered much during these evil days, but she seems to have retained something of her old independent character, for when King Alfred decided to repair her ruined walls he halted first of all at Chelsea, some miles upstream, and there perfected his plans. Later it is probable that he made his headquarters there from time to time, but his strenuous life

Dragon-prowed ships

The terror of the Londoners in the ninth century

From an illuminated Manuscript

left him little leisure for long tarrying anywhere. No sovereign has ever been crowned within the boundaries of the City. This is all the more curious because in Anglo-Saxon and Norman times the London Witenagemot, the already traditional and influential Citizens' Council, more than once asserted and exercised the right to declare who should be King. This Council, called sometimes the 'Witenagemot', sometimes simply the 'Witan', was an Anglo-

Saxon idea, the most valuable contribution they made to the future weal of England, for in it was the germ of Parliamentary Government.

There is in the noisy City of to-day a street called 'Coleman Street'. Nothing in its appearance reminds you of Anglo-Saxon London; yet in the year 857 King Alfred's brother-in-law, Burgred of Mercia, granted to Alban, Bishop

An Anglo-Saxon King presiding over a Witenagemot

These Witans were the forerunners of Parliament. Many, though not all, of them were held in London

From an illuminated Manuscript. British Museum

of Worcester, 'a little cabbage garden' on that very spot, and it was the 'straet' of 'Coelmund' even then—so closely are the ancient and the modern entwined.

Unfortunately all the Anglo-Saxon Kings were not of Alfred's mettle. At the end of the tenth century lived that proverbially foolish creature, Ethelred, nicknamed the 'Unready' because of his reluctance to follow 'rede'—that is, good counsel. Then, says the chronicler, 'in the year 994 came Anlof and Sweyn to London with ninety-four ships, constantly attacking the town and trying to set it on fire:

but they sustained more harm and evil than they ever dreamed any townsfolk might do unto them.'

The Danish King, Sweyn of the Forked Beard, having twice failed to capture London by assault, laid siege so stubbornly to the city that at last the citizens accepted him for their King. A week later he was dead, and two Witans were summoned, one in London and one at Southampton. The first elected Edmund, nick-named 'Ironside', Ethelred's valiant son; the second preferred Canute, the equally valiant son of Sweyn. According to the ancient Scandinavian saga Olaf, King of Norway, came with a fleet to help Ethelred against Sweyn, and, finding London Bridge a troublesome barrier, passed strong cables round the wooden piles, fastened these to his ships, and by bidding his men row as hard as they could downstream, brought the whole structure tumbling into the Thames.

> *London Bridge is broken down,*
> *Gold is won and high renown.*

So sang the Norse poet, thereby providing the first line of a nursery rhyme for future generations of English children; but there is no solid foundation in history for the picturesque story. What is certain is that when Canute appeared in the Thames estuary with a large fleet two years later the Bridge was still there, and still such a strong barrier that he had to dig trenches on the south bank and have his boats hauled along in order to by-pass it. Even then he could not capture the city. In the end the two claimants had to come to terms, the Dane ruling to the north and the Anglo-Saxon to the south, and the survivor to unite both under one crown. Edmund's death in 1016 left Canute supreme. The Witan met in London, and accepted him as King. He then shook hands heartily with all present: after which he exacted a tribute equal to some £10,500 in modern currency.

The Londoners never had any cause to regret their decision. Under his strong if stern rule they never ceased to prosper. Everybody has heard the story of how, in order to rebuke his flattering courtiers, he commanded the tide to rise no higher; but not everybody knows that one traditional scene of the incident was the brink of the Thames at Lambeth, and not any spot on the sea shore.[1] In 1023 London saw a

Canute and his Queen

He was chosen King at a Witan held in London
From the register of Hyde Abbey, Winchester

surprising sight: King Canute walking behind the coffin of St. Alphege as it was borne from a humble grave in St. Paul's to a golden shrine at Canterbury. It was an act of royal reparation, for it was the Danes who eleven years before had battered the holy man to death with beef-bones because he refused to lay upon his flock the burden of paying the ransom demanded by those who had taken him captive.

Winchester was still the capital of England, but London was now the largest city. To her busy harbour came ships bearing wine and fish from Normandy, timber from the

[1] Some Chroniclers say Westminster, some Southampton, others merely the 'shore.'

Baltic, spices from far-off Arabia. In exchange her merchants exported corn, hides, wool and honey. A folkmoot, or people's council, met every week in the precincts of St. Paul's. There was a Sheriff or Shire-reeve; there was a Port-Reeve, responsible to the King for the collection of taxes and the governance of the City. Spiritual affairs were under the rule of the Bishop. And a most important point—the Sheriff and the Port-Reeve were answerable for their doings to no man but the King.

To show their peaceful intentions foreign merchants approaching by land blew horns: those coming up the river sang sea-shanties. It all sounds quite gay. But there were episodes of savage cruelty in the story, too, as when the Anglo-Saxons massacred many of the Danes who formed a little colony near where the Church of St. Clement Danes—the 'Oranges and Lemons' church—now stands.

The Witan was called upon to make a momentous decision early in 1066, when the pious Edward, known as Edward the Confessor, died leaving no children. The only representative of Alfred's line was Edgar Atheling, a mere lad, most of whose youth had been spent in Hungary. William, Duke of Normandy, the dead King's cousin on his mother's side, claimed that he had been named as the next heir, and that Harold, Earl of Wessex, knew it well. This Harold denied. He declared that it was he whom his brother-in-law, King Edward, had chosen; and it was he whom the Witan chose.

Breathless days followed. Harold had no choice but to hurry northward to meet Harold Hardrada, King of Norway, who had invaded Yorkshire and whom he defeated and slew at Stamford Bridge. Before his faithful Londoners saw him again Duke William had disembarked an army on the Sussex coast.

Only for six days did Harold tarry at Westminster before,

at the head of a weary and diminished host, he set out on the
way to the sea. Ansgar, Sheriff of London, went with him
and a detachment of stout-hearted London men. They
fought valiantly on the losing side at Hastings, where many
of them fell. Ansgar himself was able to struggle home,
desperately wounded, with the news that King Harold lay

*Hoisting the weathercock on the new
Abbey of Westminster,* 1065

*It was later to show the direction of the wind that blew the Norman fleet
to England*

From the Bayeux Tapestry

dead on the field and Duke William was victorious. The
bell of St. Paul's clanged to summon the Witan, and this
time young Edgar Atheling was chosen. Then the citizens
began to make ready as best they might for the mass attack
which seemed certain to follow. A whole month went by.
Winter deepened and darkened over the land. And still the
terrible Conqueror did not appear with his archers and his
cavalry before the walls of London.

CHAPTER II

Monarchs, Merchants, Seafarers, Saints

THE winter days grew darker and shorter, and there was great fear in London. As yet no Normans with shaven faces and tunics of chain-mail had appeared before the walls, but on the opposite bank of the Thames angry red flames leapt up when they burned the little town of Southwark to ashes: and presently word came that instead of making the direct assault for which the citizens were preparing the terrible Conqueror was drawing round them a circle which would tighten as time passed.

It was the season of Advent, when no coronation might take place, and young Edgar Atheling was therefore so far a King only in name. The Londoners began to ask themselves whether the best way might not be to make their peace with Duke William. The Witan met again, the same Witan which had loudly acclaimed the Anglo-Saxon Prince. Knowing that the ring of fire and ruin was closing round London, they decided to invite the Duke to be crowned King of England. Their decision does not seem to have been challenged by Edgar Atheling, who resembled his great-grandfather, Ethelred the Unready, rather than his grandfather, Edmund Ironside.

Duke William was at Berkhamsted when messengers came from the Witan inviting him to be King.

'Let the Atheling come hither to me,' said the Duke. 'And let certain citizens of London come also. I will be as good a lord to them as ever my kinsman King Edward was.'

They came; and though not all of them could understand the Norman-French language in which the tall, broad-shouldered, keen-eyed stranger spoke to them, his looks and gestures made it plain that he wished them no evil. When Edgar Atheling knelt in homage he was raised up and kissed on the cheek.

None the less William did not immediately trust himself in the midst of the Anglo-Saxon citizens of London. He sent first a body of men to start building a stronghold on Thames-side, east of St. Paul's, partly as a warning to the people, partly as a place of refuge in case of tumults. At a spot where Alfred the Great had planted a similar though smaller fortress in a bastion of the old Roman Wall, they dug deep trenches and raised temporary wooden walls. Some ten years later those wooden walls were replaced by a formidable tower of flint and stone, palace, stronghold and prison all in one; the Tower of London.

On Christmas Day, 1066, a cold, snow-showery day, William, first of that name, was crowned in the Abbey of Westminster. Then began his heavy task of changing the whole shape and colour of English life, that process of 'Normanizing' which gave to England a new royal dynasty, a new language, new laws, and a new greatness such as she had never known before.

One of the first deeds of his reign was to grant a charter to London, promising that the citizens should be under the same laws 'as in King Edward's day'; that every child should be his father's heir; and that he 'would not suffer any man to do them wrong.'

That charter, written in the Anglo-Saxon tongue, is still preserved in Guildhall. It is one of the most momentous documents in English history—and it is only six inches long.

When William's time came to die he remembered the poor of London and bequeathed to them a thousand pounds of silver—a bequest duly paid over by his red-faced, fierce-tempered son and successor, William Rufus.

The Norman Kings continued to respect the ancient liberties of London; yet, curiously enough, it was under John, the worst of the Plantagenets, that the first Court of Aldermen was set up, 'five and twenty of the more discreet men, of the City, sworn to take counsel on behalf of the City',

Anglo-Saxons at dinner

No plates, only one cup, but an elaborate table-cloth

British Museum

together with the Mayor. And in a community where Norman French was the language of law and commerce these men bore the definitely Anglo-Saxon title of 'Aldermen'—the 'elder men'.

London flourished. But if a citizen of Londinium Augusta had returned to his old home he would have found little to admire. No pillared Basilica now, no stately Forum, no villas with tessellated pavements of many colours and no central heating! The only stone-built erections in sight would be the Tower, St. Paul's cathedral, and some religious foundations; for the rest, nothing but narrow, irregular streets bordered with thatched wooden houses in which the only source of warmth was a smoky open hearth.

A twelfth-century chronicler described London as 'merry in her sports', and merry indeed she must have been. Boys played football in the streets. Prosperous merchants mounted their nags to hunt the wild boar and the fallow deer in Epping Forest and on Highgate Hill. In the open spaces such as Moorfields the young men raced, leaped, practised archery, danced, played bowls and trap-ball, while their elders sauntered on the green turf and indulgently watched their sports. In winter, when the marshy flats were frozen over, people swooped to and fro upon skates made of sheeps' bones.

It had needed great efforts on the part of Boadicea to burn Londinium to the ground; but the ramshackle later dwellings were constantly destroyed by devastating fires, and even St. Paul's did not always escape. The magnificent cathedral begun in the last years of the eleventh century rose from the blackened ashes of an earlier and smaller church which was itself built on the site of a yet earlier one which had perished by fire. Monarchs and Mayors strove long and energetically to deter the citizens from building wooden or lath-and-plaster houses roofed with thatch; but it was not until the Great Fire of 1666 that brick and stone replaced timber throughout the City.

On the feast of St. Thomas, December 21st, 1118, many houses round about Cheapside were burned to the ground. Among these was the house of Gilbert Becket, a prosperous Anglo-Norman merchant whose wife had that very day given birth to a son destined to fill all Europe with his renown. The child was named after the Apostle upon whose festival he had come into a frosty and frightening world. In after years the whole of Christendom honoured him as Thomas of Canterbury, Saint and Martyr, but in his wordly days before King Henry the Second insisted on making him an Archbishop, he loved to call himself Thomas 'of London'. There is preserved in the Record Office an impression of his seal, made when he was at the height of his glory, and bearing the inscription *Ecce Sigillam Thomae de Lond*—behold the seal of Thomas of London.

To Gilbert Foliot, Bishop of Hereford, this remarkable man wrote: 'that the City of London surpasses in grandeur all the other cities of the Kingdom is well known . . . for the business of the whole realm is transacted therein; it is the residence of the sovereign and frequented more than any other by his nobles.' The Londoners were aware that the King's favourite was proud to call himself one of them. They must have followed with interest, sometimes possibly with alarm, the strange course of his career, first as Chancellor, high in royal regard, then as Archbishop, defending the rights of the Church against the encroachments of a King who was his friend no longer. When he came among them for the last time in the year of his death they advanced three miles beyond the city walls to welcome him. With all other Christian folk, but with a very personal sense of pity and horror, they shuddered at the news that he had been butchered by four Knights upon the altar-steps of his own cathedral.

Though the Apostle Paul had always been London's patron saint the Londoners decided within fifty years of Becket's martyrdom to commend to *his* especial protection the city of his birth. They had a new Common Seal designed, showing him in vestments and mitre, enthroned upon a rainbow-shaped arch and raising his hand in benediction. On either side kneels a little group of long-gowned citizens; beneath can be seen the towers and spires of a London which already contained more than a hundred churches. The Latin motto encircling the seal reads, *Me who gave thee birth cease not, O Thomas, to protect*. Six years after his death, when the erection of a new London Bridge was begun, an exquisite little chapel dedicated to his memory was placed in the very centre, to remind all who passed over or under that Thomas, Archbishop and Martyr, was also a loyal Londoner. Did he not once knock down a tower which a stubborn King was building against the wishes of the people?

St. Thomas of Canterbury—and of London

Londoner born, and proud of it

Common Seal of the City. Guildhall Museum

The Conqueror's youngest son, the bookish Henry the First, confirmed by charter the ancient rights of the city, and added new privileges. The Londoners, he declared, should have no overlord but the King: their Sheriffs should be elected by themselves instead of being chosen by him or his successors; their powers were made to stretch beyond their circling walls, for thenceforth they might 'farm' the county of Middlesex; and they had hunting rights not only throughout that county but as far as the Chilterns on one side and as far as St. Mary Cray in Kent on the other. As late as the reign of Elizabeth the First the Lord Mayor and Aldermen went fox-hunting on Highbury Hill and killed a fox in Cripplegate.

Lying at the end of the great trade-route from Constantinople and the Near East, London attracted commerce as if by a natural magnetic 'pull'. Spices, coats of mail, rich silks, fine linens, strong sweet wines were unloaded daily upon her quays. Of all these things the reigning sovereign had 'first pick', and it was one of the duties of the Sheriff to attend him while he was making his choice. The Londoners came next, and finally the people of Winchester and Oxford were permitted to choose.

There was one respect at least in which the imaginary visitor from Londinium Augusta would now find his old home changed for the better. Each house of any importance had a patch of garden, large or small, and the sweet scent of roses and lilies, mint, southernwood and sage struggled with the far-from-sweet odours rising from the unpaved streets where filth was allowed to gather, rubbish was piled up, and ducks and pigs wandered at will. Certain pigs had bells round their necks, and these no man might drive away, as they belonged to the monastic order of St. Antony, housed near what is now Threadneedle Street, but when it was found that some unscrupulous pig-owners hung bells on *their* pigs to claim for them the same privilege the Mayor took appropriate action to put a stop to this fraud. When distinguished visitors were expected sudden desperate efforts were made to cleanse the roadways, which were then hastily strewn with sand or straw; but in general the dirt and dust and stench were such as a modern Londoner could not even imagine.

Through the medieval City flowed what have been called the Lost Rivers, those tributaries of the Thames which, rising on the northern heights, are now imprisoned in pipes and sewers or have vanished altogether. The Fleet, from which Fleet Street takes its name, followed a zig-zag course and joined the greater river near Blackfriars. The little Walbrook, dividing the two low hills upon which Roman London was built, was not vaulted over till the fifteenth century. The Westbourne is still visible at one point: it feeds the Serpentine in Hyde Park. The name of Stratford (Street Ford) Place, Oxford Street, marks the spot where the Tyburn crossed that highway. It turned a water-mill for the monks of Westminster before losing itself in the Thames near Vauxhall. Dwellers upon the banks of these streams were constantly being scolded by the Mayor for allowing them to become silted up with refuse and well into the eighteenth century the terrible state of the Fleet Ditch was proverbial.

When William the Atheling, only son of Henry the First, perished in the wreck of the *White Ship*, Londoners realized with dismay that no man knew who next might wear the crown. The King's only daughter, the Empress Matilda (sometimes called 'Maud' for short) was far away in the German Empire, where she had been brought up, but his nephew Stephen had been bred in England. The time would come when they must choose between the two and it was not difficult to guess where their choice would fall.

Meanwhile the King, his court, his capital, and indeed the whole land, lay under a dark cloud of sorrow. He had always been a stern man, but after the death of William the Atheling, men said that he never smiled again. In earlier days he had been seen to smile—sometimes even heard to laugh—at the merry quips of a certain Rahere, who may have been his official jester, or perhaps the wittiest member of his royal household.

Like many other people connected with the Court Rahere was so deeply shocked by the tragedy of the *White Ship* that he resolved to go on a pilgrimage to Rome. All pilgrims did not set forth in this solemn mood; many of them went simply for the fun of seeing strange lands in company with many-coloured groups of fellow-pilgrims; but in the mind of Rahere was nothing but penitence and piety. While he

Tomb of Prior Rahere

Jester, monk, and founder of London's most ancient Hospital

In the church of St. Bartholomew the Great, Smithfield

was in Rome he fell sick of a fever, and in his delirium he had a vision of the Apostle Bartholomew, who promised him that he would recover if on his return to England he built in the place called Smoothfield[1] a hospital for the sick poor dedicated to the Apostle himself. Rahere vowed that he

[1] Later known as Smithfield.

would obey. He did recover; and when he was safely back in London he set to work to fulfil his vow.

The King readily granted him a tract of land upon the rather dreary spot chosen by St. Bartholomew, and gifts of all kinds soon came pouring in. Rahere became a monk—he was the first Prior of the Priory of St. Bartholomew's, Smithfield—and people thronged to hear him preach, for his sermons were as witty as his worldly talk had once been. Children loved him. The small boys and girls of the parish found it a delightful new game to carry little baskets of sand or gravel for him when the foundations of the new church and hospital were being laid out. The seafarers of London loved the place too, and when they returned safely from perilous voyages they offered silver models of their ships to be hung before the high altar.

Those silver ships vanished long ago, but the choir or eastern part of the church still stands and is the most ancient —and the most beautiful—sacred building within the line of the old city walls. There you may see Prior Rahere's tomb, on which lies his carven image in his monk's habit: a little monk holding a large book kneels on one side of him, and at his feet kneels an angel holding a shield. Not far away the great hospital of St. Bartholomew, familiarly called 'Bart's', still carries on the noble work of healing begun by him more than eight hundred years ago.

After the death of the unsmiling King it became necessary to decide who should reign in his stead. In spite of the fact that Stephen had twice sworn allegiance to his cousin, the Empress Matilda, as 'Lady of England', he did not hesitate to accept the crown when the citizens of London, asserting their ancient right, chose him as King. They knew him well, and they thought well of him; they had no mind to bow the knee to a Queen Regnant and what they had heard of the Empress and her second husband, Geoffrey of Anjou, nicknamed 'Plantagenet',[1] did little to reassure them. She was a masterful woman; he was a foolish man; they had a small son who might possibly grow up to resemble them both. So the Londoners backed Stephen, though they were not pleased when he filled their city with foreign soldiers whom he had hired to fight in support of his not-very-good claim; and they soon realized that he was not the stuff of which a strong King is made.

Years passed; the ding-dong struggle went on, and in fulness of time Henry, the son of Geoffrey and Matilda, appeared in England, and succeeded in persuading Stephen to promise that he and none other should follow him upon the throne. Once again the Londoners were ill-pleased. 'We will not have a robber from Anjou for our King,' said they; but when in due course Henry the Second was crowned they changed their note.

One of his first actions was to send away Stephen's foreign hirelings; then he set about ruling his new realm with a firm hand.

During the thirty-five years that his reign lasted Henry spent in England less than fourteen all told. Yet under the rule of his ministers London prospered, growing in wealth, influence and outward loveliness. She had now at least 146 churches, not all built of stone but all of them lit by stained glass windows and surmounted by belfries which filled the air with their chimes. Her walls, ungrimed as yet by coal-smoke, shone pearly white in the clear air.

In the year 1176 a new bridge of stone was built near the site of an older one of elmwood but a little farther west. A priest called Peter de Colechurch was bridge-master, and from the circumstance that Henry the Second contributed to the cost with the proceeds of a tax on wool grew the saying that 'London Bridge is built on wool-packs'. Even

---

[1] From the *planta genista* or broomflower which he took as his badge.

the graceless King John levied tolls on foreign merchants to help towards the maintenance of the structure, which was twenty feet wide and rested upon nineteen pointed arches.

Meanwhile the lines dividing Normans from Saxons were gradually growing fainter. A new people, rightly called the 'English'[1] were coming into existence.

The second Plantagenet, that fierce, valiant and romantic figure, Richard of the Lion Heart, seems to have thought of London chiefly as a place in which to borrow money. During his long absences from England he appointed Longchamps, Bishop of Ely, to exercise the royal authority—and to squeeze as much gold as possible out of the resentful citizens. Two years before his crowning Richard had pledged himself to join the other Christian princes who were planning the Third Crusade, and no sooner had the crown been placed upon his handsome auburn head than he began to look about him in quest of the funds needed to finance this great adventure. He knew well where would be the most promising place to look. 'I would sell London,' he once exclaimed, 'if I could find someone to buy!'

It was indeed London gold which helped to pay for his magnificent ship, *Trenc-la-Mer* or Cleave the Sea, for his famous flame-coloured charger, Flavel, and for the scarlet saddle embroidered with golden leopards which so dazzled the people of Joppa when he rode in triumph through the town.

England paid dearly for the privilege of having a Crusader King; and when on his homeward way from that luckless enterprise he was captured and held for ransom by the German Emperor, the good folk of London were compelled to contribute towards that ransom a sum equal to two million pounds in modern currency. His reign was none the less memorable in the history of the City, for it was in

[1] Not, strictly speaking, 'British' until the Act of Union in 1707.

1193 that in any document still existing the chief citizen was first called the 'Mayor': 'Lord Mayor' he would not be called until the very end of the Plantagenet period. It was under the name of 'Mayor' that he was appointed one of the official treasurers of the royal ransom-money.

During Richard's absence his graceless younger brother John had been plotting busily against him. He was clever enough to make use of the loathing felt by the Londoners for the Bishop of Ely; and it so fell out that in October, 1191, the Barons of the realm and the principal citizens of London held a meeting in St. Paul's Cathedral at which they deposed the Bishop and accepted John as Regent in Richard's stead.

John on his side swore to maintain the ancient liberties of the City and to recognize its institution as an independent, self-governing *communia*, or corporation governed by a Mayor. London thus became the first municipal corporation in England, serving as a model to the twenty-eight lesser medieval towns which afterwards received charters. Richard the First was a ready granter of charters—they brought money into his almost empty treasury. At an early date the Mayor and Aldermen maintained a force of armed men, available either for police work or for service in the field. These were later known as the 'Armed Bands', and later still as the 'Trained Bands', and they were destined to play an important part in England's story. The London Territorial Regiments may be said to represent them in our own day, and on the civilian side the City and Metropolitan Police.

The return of Richard the First from prison was one of the occasions when the streets were hastily cleansed and such pigs as had no bells about their necks were driven away. As the King, pale and haggard from the hardships of his captivity, rode through the City, flowers were strewn before his horse's hoofs.

'My lord King,' said one of the German nobles who had

come to receive the ransom-money, 'if my master the Emperor could see this sight, he would demand a larger ransom!'

Richard soon went overseas again, but in his absence the officers representing him were soon at their old tricks of exacting taxes and tolls with ever-increasing harshness and greed. A number of angry Londoners rose in rebellion under a certain William FitzOsbert, nicknamed William 'of the Long Beard'. He was a goldsmith by trade, had gone crusading against the Moors in Portugal, and had also been favoured with a vision of St. Thomas of Canterbury. Perhaps on this account Archbishop Hubert Walter, acting for the absent King, dealt mildly with him at first; but the City authorities, disliking violence in any form, had their own ideas and hanged him on the gallows near Smithfield Priory.

A year later two of the abuses which most annoyed the citizens were removed. The Wardens of the Tower were forbidden to ask more than the lawful toll-money from ships coming up the Thames and all the weirs in the river were removed. These weirs were useful to fishermen but most inconvenient for trading vessels.

Richard died as he had lived—a true figure of chivalry; there was nothing chivalrous about his brother John. The Londoners, it is true, found him at first an uncommonly affable Prince, and his rich raiment, his crimson mantle sewn with sapphires and pearls, his white damask tunic girdled with garnets and sapphires, his white gloves set one with a sapphire and the other with a ruby, appealed to their taste for splendour. But this happy state of affairs did not last long. What respect could London feel for a King whose folly flung away most of the French territories inherited from his father—territories equal to three-fifths of modern France? What hope had they of spiritual comfort when their sovereign lord quarrelled so violently with their

Holy Father the Pope, that the whole land was laid for four years under an Interdict? At such times Christian marriage and Christian burial were denied, though infants might be baptized and Mass was celebrated four times a year. Belfries were silent, churches were empty, thistles and poppies sprang up in churchyards.

It seems hardly surprising that when the Pope invited Philip Augustus of France to invade and annex England, the English, well accustomed to be ruled by Kings of foreign birth, should have agreed, feeling no doubt that none could be worse than the one they already had.

John was frightened: he grovelled. London had no use now for this miserable image of royalty, and he seems to have hated the City as heartily as the City hated him. In the nineteenth year of his evil reign Barons and Bishops, gathering once more in St. Paul's Cathedral, swore an oath to put an end to the evils of John's rule. The Barons spoke Norman-French; so did the Bishops, when they were not speaking Latin; but in character they were all English, as we understand the word to-day, and Archbishop Stephen Langton, the leader of the Church Party, was neither Norman nor Saxon but an Englishman, born and bred of the two races.

From this meeting in the still fire-scarred London cathedral grew one of the greatest events in our history—Magna Carta; but at first the only demand made was that John should renew the Charter granted by his great-grandfather, Henry the First.

Events followed fast. John twisted and turned, offered (not for the first time) to hand over his dominions to the Pope in exchange for papal support against the Barons, professed great anxiety to take the Cross and fight in Palestine: but he had to choose between fighting the Barons and the Bishops in the open field or doing what they desired.

The Londoners dug a new and deep moat round their rather battered city wall. Robert FitzWalter, Baron of Dunmow, hereditiary 'Banneret' or commander of London's armed forces, was created 'Marshal of the Army of God and Holy Church'. He lived in Baynard's Castle, one of the great

Archbishop Stephen Langton

'*Neither Norman nor Saxon but an Englishman*'

From his Seal. British Museum

fortress-palaces rising along the south side of the Strand, and could therefore claim to be in some sense a Londoner.

Early in the summer of 1215 it seemed as if open warfare would be the only way out. The Barons, who had massed their forces north of London, attacked certain royal strongholds but they dared not risk a direct attack on the greatest royal stronghold of all—the Tower of London, where the King had taken up his quarters. Then a message came to them which changed the whole course of history.

It came from the citizens of London, who sent word that if the Barons wished to enter the City they would find Aldgate unbarred. When the King heard that the Barons were hot on his heels, he fled to Windsor. Those determined men did not forget what they owed to the Londoners. The Charter to which John gave his reluctant assent at Runnymede on June 15, 1215, contained sixty-nine clauses or conditions; and the fifteenth of these ran . . . 'the City of London shall have all its ancient Liberties and free Customs as well by Land as by Water'.

But England's (and London's) troubles were not ended at Runnymede. The King wriggled his way out of his promises and the Barons in desperation invited Prince Louis, eldest son of Philip Augustus, King of France, to come over and take possession of the English throne.

He came—in May, 1216: he remained for about a year, during which his hired troops occupied London. Some of the Londoners liked him well enough; others, after the somewhat mysterious death of the graceless John in October, 1216, ranged themselves with those who upheld the claims of John's young son, Prince Henry, now Henry the Third. It was a curious position, for many of the Magna Carta Barons sided with Louis and thus became an anti-patriotic group in the land. Then one of the most remarkable men of the pro-English party, William Marshal, Earl of Pembroke, was chosen 'ruler of the King and of the Kingdom'. He took the field against Louis of France, one of whose chief Captains he slew with his own hands. In due course Louis withdrew to his own dominions, and under William Marshal's strong and just rule London and all England prospered.

Londoners knew him well by sight, a tall, athletic man, his face bronzed by exposure to the weather, and his air so noble that, as a chronicler of the time declared, 'he might have been the Emperor of Rome'. In his earlier days he had journeyed to the Holy Land, 'where in two years he wrought such great deeds as no one else might have wrought in seven'. At the Coronation of Richard Lion Heart he had carried the golden sceptre of England while the Mayor carried the crystal sceptre of London.

Shortly before his death in the year 1219 this fine states-man-warrior joined the order of military monks known as the Templars—the Knights of the Temple at Jerusalem. Wearing their characteristic garb, the great white mantle with the eight-pointed crimson cross on one shoulder, he was duly buried in their noble circular church on Thames-side. He did not live long enough to be disappointed by the young King's folly, extravagance and feebleness. Like his father John and his uncle Richard, Henry was always trying to squeeze more and yet more money out of London. He even called upon the Sheriffs to pay fourpence a day towards the upkeep of his pet bear, and to supply a cord for it when it desired to swim in the river. It was he who moved the royal menagerie from Woodstock to the Tower, and there it remained till 1834. During all those six centuries it was a popular sight—hence the saying 'to go and see the lions', which has long outlasted the Tower menagerie.

The Jewish community were expected to pay his wax-chandlers and his wine-merchants; the Jewish quarter of the City was sacked and plundered during his reign and stones from the ruins were used to repair the City walls. Many innocent Jews as well as many guilty ones (and a few Christ-ians) were cruelly punished for the grave crime of 'clipping' the coinage—that is to say, reducing the weight and value of the coins by clipping the edges and then melting down for their own benefit the metal thus obtained. Yet the Children of Israel kept their foothold in England despite persecution and public hatred. There were more than a million of them when they were expelled by Edward the First in 1291.

London was now a lovely sight,
A City blazoned like a missal-book,
    Black with oaken gables carven and enscrolled.

She prospered; yet she was not at peace, for the King's French-born brother-in-law, Simon de Montfort, Earl of

Simon de Montfort

London was fined 20,000 marks for siding with him against Henry the Third

                    From a window in Chartres Cathedral

Leicester, was making desperate efforts to bring about certain much needed reforms. It was for fear of de Montfort and his followers that Henry and his foolish Queen, Eleanor of

¹ Alfred Noyes: *Tales of the Mermaid Tavern.*

Provence, took refuge in the Tower, but she soon decided that Windsor would be an even safer retreat, and so set off up the river in her red-oared barge. The strength and swiftness of the current between the piers of London Bridge often made it a difficult and even dangerous matter to get a boat through. People would peer over to watch boatmen 'shooting the rapids', and some of these idlers recognized the flag on Eleanor's barge. Thereupon, says an old chronicler, 'sundrie Londiners' not only 'cryed owt upon her with reprochfull words but also threw myre and stones at her'. Her husband and her long-legged elder son were furious.

Led by their Mayor, Thomas FitzThomas, the majority of the 'Londiners' were hot on de Montfort's side. The minority, headed by a pepperer named John de Gisors, barred the gates of London Bridge against the Earl and threw the keys into the river. FitzThomas then caused the gates to be broken down, and in de Montfort came. Many London lads later followed the Frenchman into Sussex and fought for him at the Battle of Lewes, though without winning much glory on the field. Edward of the Long Shanks, remembering how 'sundrie Londiners' had insulted his mother, concentrated his attack upon their part of the line with deadly effect, thereby leaving the main body of the royal army unsupported and enabling his father's enemy to win the day.

A year later the tables were turned at the Battle of Evesham where de Montfort perished and the cause for which he stood was, for the time being, overthrown. London was fined 20,000 marks for siding with him; FitzThomas was summoned to Windsor Castle and never seen again; and for five years the City was ruled by the Constable of the Tower instead of by a Mayor of its own choosing. Then, at the request of the Queen and her son, the King restored that ancient right of choice, stubbornly claimed since Anglo-Saxon days.

Another link with those days was—and is—the City Sceptre, a rod of grooved crystal one foot six inches long, adorned with bands of pearls and sapphires set in gold, and carried by the Chief Magistrate of London at the Coronation of every English sovereign from time immemorial. It was carried by Sir Rupert de la Bère before Queen Elizabeth the Second in June, 1953, but as there are now no banquets

The Crystal Sceptre

One of London's most ancient treasures.

Still in the possession of the City

in Westminster Hall he and the Aldermen could not serve her as cupbearers on that occasion—another ancient privilege.

When Londoners elected a new Mayor they proceeded in great state to Westminster to obtain the royal assent. If the King were absent, the Barons of the Exchequer represented him. These 'ridings' were the origin of the modern Lord Mayor's Show, but the Lord Chief Justice now acts for the sovereign, and the scene is at the Law Courts instead of at the Palace of Westminster. The brief ceremony itself is much the same as it was in Plantagenet days.

CHAPTER III

Turbulent Years

LONDONERS were proud of their city. It had been founded, they said, by a Trojan Prince named Brut, and by him called 'New Troy'. Nobody knew that this legend grew out of a dim remembrance of the Trinovantes, the Celtic tribe of pre-Roman times.

In the thirteenth century Mathew Paris, a monk of St. Albans, drew a little sketch of *la Cité de Lundres*, a walled City pricked with towers. St. Paul's rises in the centre, with *la Tour* on the left, and Lambeth and Westminster on the right. Between them flows *la grante rivière de la Tamise*. One can make out Aldersgate, Cripplegate, Ludgate and Billingsgate. Every gate in the wall was fortified and guarded, but the room or rooms over it would be used as sort of 'flatlet'. The Town Crier lived at Aldersgate, the Chief Carver at Bishopsgate, the poet Chaucer for a little while at Aldgate. Being responsible for the upkeep of the gate called his, the Bishop of London could claim one stick from each cartload of faggots passing through.

No houses are shown in Brother Mathew's drawing, and no churches except the cathedral; but the houses were many and small and the churches many and large within the girdle of the ancient walls. In the ground-floor chamber of these two-storeyed wooden dwellings merchants displayed their wares and craftsmen plied their craft. In the room above (there was seldom more than one) the owner of the house lived with his family. Among the thatched roofs silver

44

blossom peeped out in May and golden apples in September. Upper storeys had to leave a space of nine feet to enable a horseman to ride by without bumping his head.

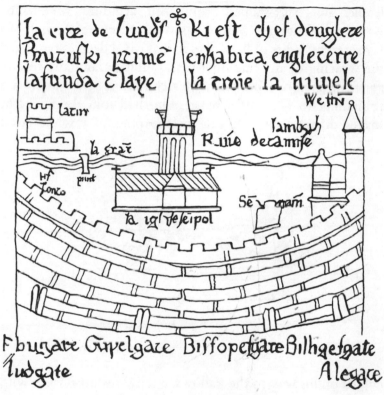

London in the Thirteenth Century

'*Brut, who first occupied England, founded the city and named it New Troy*'

From the Chronicle of Matthew Paris

The ghost of a Roman Londoner might have marvelled to see so much prosperity side by side with so little real comfort.

The *grante rivière* was thronged with ships. All day long

the narrow, twisting streets were crowded by people; cowled monks, shaven priests, long-gowned merchants with bronze-clasped pouches hanging from their girdles, shrill-voiced 'prentice lads, pilgrims, minstrels, knights in leather suits rust-stained from their armour. Merchants' wives and daughters were so fond of following the fashions favoured by ladies of high degree that royal decrees regulated the wearing of any furs finer than rabbit or lambkin, or any garment lined or trimmed with rich silk. There was always something to be seen: a baker who had sold short-weight loaves dragged on a hurdle to the pillory, a white-faced

A Baker on his way to the Pillory

The 'short-weight' loaf is hung round his neck

From an illuminated Manuscript

culprit on his way to the gallows, a religious procession with fuming incense and billowing banners, a wedding party singing as they went. Better still were the royal pageants. When Edward the First returned from Palestine for his crowning, gold and silver coins showered from the windows; and when he came in triumph after some victory over the wild Welsh or the stubborn Scots the City Guilds vied with each other as to who best should welcome him.

On one such occasion the Fishmongers, forty-six of them, rode through the streets upon steeds tricked out with flippers and moustaches to represent 'sea-horses', the medieval name for a walrus. Huge models of salmon and sturgeon, gay with gilding, were drawn by teams of eight land-horses. There were still salmon in the Thames and already a sturgeon was regarded as a dish for the table of a King.

Edward of the Longshanks was a ruler as well as a warrior. He fostered trade and protected merchants. When he

Great Seal of Edward the First

With lion-cubs at his feet and lions on his shield

British Museum

imposed heavy taxes he explained, even with tears, why the money was needed and how sorry he was. The Dean of St. Paul's was so indignant when the royal tax-gatherers raided the cathedral treasury, he went to Westminster and craved speech with the King. The prayer was granted; but the eye of Edward glared at him so fiercely, he fell dead at Edward's feet.

Though the City clashed sometimes with its long-legged monarch, the citizens grieved with him over the death of his Queen, the beloved Eleanor of Castile, and stood sadly watching the funeral procession as it moved through the streets on its way to Westminster. Her coffin rested a while in Cheapside, and a beautiful sculptured cross later marked the spot. The last of fourteen 'Eleanor crosses' was at the village of Charing,[1] thereafter called 'Charing Cross'.

As so often happens, a strong father was followed by a weak son. Edward the Second, foppish and feeble, was quite unfit to cope with the Scots, especially after they had found in Robert the Bruce a leader worthy of a valiant people fighting to be free. When Bruce pressed southward and threatened the important Border stronghold of Berwick-upon-Tweed the City sent a detachment of armed men to share in the vain English effort to save it from the Scots.

One of the outstanding figures in this unhappy reign was Walter de Stapledon, Bishop of Exeter, *Custos* or Warden of London and treasurer of the realm. Exeter Street, running down from the Strand to the north bank of the Thames, marks the site of the great palace once the town residence of the Bishops of that see. Bishop Walter did his utmost to guide aright the wilful successor of his old master, Edward the First, but Edward the Second would not be guided. Foolish in his choice of friends, the mocking Piers Gaveston and the greedy Despensers, the young King was also most unfortunate in his Queen, Isabel, sometimes called the She-Wolf of France. She had tried to cultivate the good-will of the City. When her son, the future Edward the Third, was born, she sent a courteous letter to inform the 'Mayor, Aldermen and Commonalty of London', whereupon, as the old records tell, they met in Guildhall, 'and carolled and showed great joy', and passed through the streets 'with great glare of torches and with trumpets and other minstrelsies.'

---

[1] Charing Cross was pulled down by the Puritans in 1647 but a modern replica stands outside the station of that name.

They were perturbed when she left her husband, taking her young son with her, and remained for two years in her native land of France. When she returned, she issued proclamations promising to remove many grievances and, incidentally, to get rid of the King's evil friends. One of these proclamations was affixed to the Cross in Cheapside, amid much popular excitement. King Edward was in the Tower, but on hearing that the proclamation had been welcomed by the people and that his wife and son were approaching London with a large force of sympathisers, he took to flight.

Bishop de Stapledon was made of sterner stuff. As Warden of the City he demanded that the keys should be handed to him 'for the preservation of peace and order'. This the Mayor and Aldermen were apparently ready to do, but as they made their way towards his palace in the Strand they were met and forcibly hustled back to Guildhall by a mob which favoured the Queen and regarded him as a tool of the detested Despensers. Hearing this, the Bishop mounted his horse and rode up the Strand towards Ludgate, apparently intending to seek sanctuary in St. Paul's; but the mob were too quick for him. They barred his way, dragged him from the saddle, hauled him to Cheapside, and there hastily and mercilessly hacked off his head. They also wrecked and looted Exeter House.

These evil deeds brought many evil things in their train. After the King had been murdered even more cruelly than the loyal de Stapledon his widow ruled the land hand-in-glove with her favourite Mortimer, and ruled it so badly that London must sometimes have regretted even so poor a Prince as her husband was. The scene soon changed when the third Edward was old enough to grasp the reins. Then again the people carolled, the trumpets clamoured, the torches flared, to greet good tidings—the birth of yet another royal baby, or the news of yet another English victory on land or sea. And then again London men-at-arms fought against the still-troublesome Scots. Wearing green hoods and cheered on by their own minstrel, they acquitted themselves valiantly at Halidon Hill, when Berwick was finally wrested from Scotland.

Merchants from many lands flourished upon Thames-side. Those from Lombardy gave Lombard Street the name it

An English Merchant of Edward the Third's Reign

A typical representative of a class growing rapidly in power

From the Ellesmere Manuscript

still bears; those from the Baltic were granted a wharf of their own for the unloading of cargoes of timber and tar, rope and resin, flax and hemp. In 1340 Edward the Third gathered together a strong naval force to cope with the French and Genoese fleets which constantly harassed and plundered English shipping in the Channel and were as troublesome to the mercantile vessels of other foreign nations as they were to those of his own subjects. London contributed three ships, of which one was called the *Jonette*, perhaps after the Captain's wife or his daughter; and a certain William Haunsard, an ex-Sheriff of the City, showed by his gallant deeds that he could wield a sword as well as a quill-pen. Sixpence a day seems a small rate of pay now, but in the fourteenth century it was the highest for ordinary seamen, and those from London were able to claim it by reason of their superior pluck and skill.

After the victory of Sluys the Narrow Seas were free for a time, but presently ships that were little better than pirate-vessels began to play havoc with English craft bearing wool to Flanders and wine from Aquitaine. These new enemies bore the flag of Castile, gay with golden castles and crimson lions, but Edward resolved that the English flag with its three golden lions on a red field should put the Castilian beasts to flight, and this was duly done in 1350 at the Battle of Lespagnols-sur-Mer (the Spaniards-on-the-sea), to the great joy of the King and the no small satisfaction of his good Londoners.

Between these two victories a grievous disaster fell upon Europe—the pestilence known as the Black Death, brought, as some folk said, by Genoese merchants from the far land of Tartary. Nearly half the population perished when in 1348 it reached England. In the country cattle strayed among the unreaped corn, ploughs rusted, thatch rotted, apples and cherries tumbled unheeded from the bough, but in London, where fresh air and water were both so hard to come by, the mortality was far heavier. Pitying the dead who were thrust into unconsecrated earth, Sir Walter de Manny, Knight of the Garter, leased a large field from St. Bartholomew's Priory and had it hallowed for Christian burial. Two hermits were to pray constantly for the souls of those who lay there.

London, like the rest of the realm, stoutly supported Edward the Third's rather flimsy claim to the crown of France, the claim whence sprang the long-drawn-out misery of the Hundred Years' War. For some time there had been an uneasy feeling that a French fleet might slip up the Thames under cover of darkness some night. Six brass cannon on rollers, four and a half hundredweight of 'pellets' and thirty-two pounds of powder were stored anxiously in Guildhall until the victories of Crécy and Poitiers caused the danger to recede. The Black Prince sent the news of Poitiers to his 'dear and much beloved people of London', and presently the Mayor and Aldermen crossed London Bridge in a proud procession to greet the Prince and the captive King of France upon the South Bank. The Prince had mounted his royal prisoner upon a handsome grey charger while he himself trotted modestly upon a small black nag.

So sorry were the Londoners for King Jean that several of the City Guilds, the Drapers, Fishmongers, Mercers and Grocers among them, contributed sums towards the enormous ransom demanded for him. He was lodged in the Palace of the Savoy, on the south side of the Strand, and thither the King and Queen came from Westminster to visit him, rowed in their great barge with its red-painted oars. The ransom was never paid, and Jean died in the midst of his kindly enemies, the people of London. Wearing black hoods and carrying tapers, many of them followed his funeral procession across the Bridge on the first stage of the slow journey to the coast of Kent.

His had been no strict captivity. On one occasion he was entertained at a banquet by Sir Henry Picard, Vintner, twice Mayor, and wealthy citizen. Picard's house was considered not unworthy to receive four Kings at once—they of England, Scotland, France and Cyprus. After dinner the guests indulged in a little gambling, and the King of Cyprus grumbled because the dice fell so seldom in his favour. Sir Henry offered to hand back all that he himself had won from him, but the Kings of France and Scotland would not hear of this. A gentleman who played games of chance, said they, must be willing to pay his losses.

Dame Picard's father was, like her husband, a vintner. Trades often ran in families, but round about that time there was a certain vintner's son who instead of following in his father's footsteps had become a page in the royal household and thereafter rose to various official employments, the Comptrollership of the Customs of the Port of London among them. This was the tenant of the room above Aldgate, Geoffrey Chaucer. Some of his neighbours may have

Edward the Third

With the lilies of France on his shield

From his Great Seal in the British Museum

heard with interest that he had actually charmed his royal patrons with verses written not in the Norman-French of courtly convention but in just such homely English[1] as they themselves spoke every day.

There were two other poets then living in London and writing in English but neither was a Londoner born. John Gower, a Kentish squire, was on friendly terms with Geoffrey Chaucer, and it is possible that in the echoing aisles of St.

[1] English was first used in the City records in 1383.

Paul's they may have unwittingly rubbed elbows with the third poet, a poor priest from the West Country, William Langland by name, who eked out a meagre existence by singing Masses for the souls of the departed. The dust of Chaucer lies at Westminster, the dust of Gower at Southwark, but no one can say where the dust of Long Will Langland lies.

In the same year that Sir Henry Picard entertained four Kings in his fine new house his own company, the Vintners, accused a certain John Penrose of selling red wine which was 'unsound and unwholesome, in deceit of the common people, in contempt of our lord the King . . . and to the grievous damage of the commonalty'. He was condemned to drink a deep draught of his own bad wine, whatever was left in the tankard being then poured over his head.

There were only too many rogues about. Some made rings, buckles and buttons of base metal, painted them to resemble gold and silver and sold them as such; brewers watered their beer; taverners put false bottoms in their tankards to make them hold less liquor than they seemed to do. Bakers put bars of iron in their loaves to make them weigh more; some metal pots were so inferior that the moment they were put on the fire they melted away. Between the wickedness of men and the watchfulness of the Mayor and Aldermen the pillory can seldom have stood empty for long.

During the last years of the reign of Edward the Third many heads must have nodded anxiously together in the busy streets of his capital, for while he lay dying in the Palace of Sheen his valiant eldest son, the Black Prince, lay dying in the Palace of Westminster. The King outlived the Prince only a year. In the meantime his grandson, Richard of Bordeaux, had been formally recognized by London as 'very Heir Apparent', and his second son, John of Gaunt, had been giving evidence of that meddlesome, masterful disposition which later caused so much trouble. He came forward as the champion of John Wyclif, a country priest who was preaching a new doctrine, namely that all authority should come from the Bible and none from the Church. This doctrine was naturally frowned upon by the great churchmen of the land, and many of Wyclif's disciples were burned alive to punish them for their 'heresy'—a punishment from which he himself was saved by the protection of John of Gaunt.

So angry was that Prince when the Bishop of London and the Mayor took sides against the reformer, he threatened to drag the Bishop out of St. Paul's cathedral by his hair and to abolish the title of 'Mayor'. Riots broke out. The City Militia, stout fellows armed with bills[1] and bows, were summoned by beat of drum, and John's palace in the Strand would have been sacked and burned if the Bishop had not generously interceded.

It would have been a wonderful house to loot, for it was full of treasures. We know that one of the beds was draped with rich white and crimson silk embroidered with a design showing a turtle-dove sitting in a golden tree.

Hardly had the aged King breathed his last when the Mayor and other leading citizens made their way to Sheen begging the eleven-year-old Richard the Second to come and take up his abode in the Tower, among his loyal subjects whose lives and fortunes were at his command. In accordance with ancient custom he would in any case have spent the eve of his Coronation within those ancient walls, and this he duly did.

On July 16, 1377, he was escorted in great state to Westminster, while bells chimed gaily and fountains ran with wine. As always on such occasions, the new monarch had to draw

---

[1] Staves with metal tips.

rein from time to time in order to admire triumphal arches, to listen to loyal compliments in rhyme, and to watch brief pageants played upon temporary scaffolds by the wayside. In honour of the Black Prince's son London made a special effort; never had there been so many arches, such elaborate pageants, such quantities of flowery verse. In consequence poor young Richard's progress was so often interrupted that it took him three hours to reach the Abbey; but one of the pageants must have pleased him, for the principal performers were four little girls about his own age. Dressed as angels, they stood on the towers of a wooden castle and showered golden flowers and gilded florins upon his head and before the hoofs of his horse. Then they climbed down, and one of them offered him wine in a cup of gold. He must have been glad of a drink, for that slow, noisy ride under the hot July sun would be thirsty work for a small boy.

Everybody understood that young Richard could not be held responsible for the deeds of his counsellors or for the heavy taxes with which the people were oppressed, but it was to him, then fourteen years of age, that a direct personal appeal was made when the men of Essex and Kent rose in rebellion in July 1381. Londoners were alarmed to learn that a huge mob was mustering in Blackheath, and they were still more alarmed when sympathizers within the City let down the drawbridge which William Walworth, the Mayor, had prudently caused to be drawn up.

The Essex rebels were led by a loud-voiced fellow, Jack Straw by name; those from Kent marched under the commands of Walter the Tiler, otherwise 'Wat Tyler', of Deptford, with whom came John Ball, an eloquent, excitable cleric whose sermons were such as to shock soberminded people as much as they inflamed the other sort. No word of treason was uttered against the King, but many wild threats were shouted against the Chancellor of the realm,

Simon of Sudbury, Archbishop of Canterbury, the Treasurer, Sir Robert Hailes, and the King's uncle, John of Gaunt.

Wat Tyler's first objective was John of Gaunt's magnificent palace in the Strand. Having killed those who sought to keep them out, mobs pillaged the richly-furnished rooms and then burned the whole palace to the ground. Next they destroyed the buildings of the Order of the Knights Hospitallers in Clerkenwell recently erected by Sir Robert Hailes.

The King was in the Tower with his mother, the Princess of Wales, the Archbishop of Canterbury, and other great folk. By whose advice no one knows, perhaps on his own initiative, he sent a message bidding the rebels retire to Mile End, where he would meet them, and hear what they had to say.

The meeting took place, and Richard, with a smiling face, promised that they should receive a new charter to redress all their wrongs. Thirty clerks were set to work that night by candlelight to make copies of this charter for distribution throughout the land, and the deputation, completely satisfied, went their way; but neither Wat Tyler nor Jack Straw had come to meet the King. As soon as Richard had quitted the Tower and set off towards Mile End, they gathered together the more violent of their followers and entered that ancient royal stronghold by force.

When the Archbishop of Canterbury and Sir Robert Hailes heard the tumult outside the walls and realized that the garrison would not be able—perhaps was not willing—to beat off the attack, they went to the Chapel of St. John in the Tower and hastily received the Sacrament for what they both knew must be the last time on earth. Wat Tyler and his men soon found them, and, declaring that they were traitors to the King, dragged them out on to Tower Hill and there brutally hacked off their heads, which they later set up over London Bridge. They also found the King's mother, who had taken refuge in her richly-curtained bed, but beyond poking the bed with their swords to make sure that no one was hidden there and giving her a few beery kisses they did her no harm.

The Princess's attendants carried her, half-fainting, to a house of hers known as the 'Wardrobe' in Carter Lane, and there she was joined by her son, who must then have regretted his mild treatment of the rebels.

Next day Wat Tyler mustered some twenty thousand of his followers on the open space before the western door of St. Bartholomew's Priory, Smithfield. In the interim there had been, as an old chronicler puts it, 'no little slaughter in the City': the mob was completely out of hand, and any goodwill the Londoners may have felt towards them had now melted away.

To Smithfield the King came for a second meeting with his rebellious subjects. Wat Tyler, shaking him cordially by the hand, bade him to be of good cheer but added threateningly that the charters promised the previous day did not go far enough. Much more was needed to satisfy the people. Everything must be free for everybody. Wat then dismounted from the shaggy pony on which he had come to the meeting-place and called for a cup of water with which he noisily rinsed his mouth. After that he called for—and drank—a mug of ale before remounting. Suddenly a voice was raised in the group of nobles, knights and squires clustering round the King. 'I know that man,' said the voice. 'He is the greatest villain and robber in all Kent.'

Wat Tyler was furious.

'By my faith,' he bellowed, 'I will never eat meat again until I have that fellow's head!'

At this critical moment the Mayor, William Walworth, rode up with twelve armed horsemen.

Thrusting himself between Wat and the King, he sternly

told the rebel to respect the royal presence. Wat's reply was an angry oath and a menacing gesture. Thereupon the Mayor drew his dagger and aimed a blow at the man's throat. One of the King's squires followed with a second blow, but the first was enough. Tyler blindly wheeled his pony round, rode a few paces, and then, with a broken cry of 'Avenge me!' tumbled dying from the saddle.

Knights Jousting

Jousts and Tournaments were often held at Smithfield or even upon London Bridge

From an illuminated manuscript. British Museum

They carried him into St. Bartholomew's Priory—you can still see the carved gateway through which he was carried—and his followers, loudly lamenting the loss of their leader, bent their bows as if about to begin a battle; but young Richard, in the true spirit of his father, the Black Prince, spurred his horse forward and cried out, 'Tyler was a traitor —I will be your leader.' He then bade them follow him to the fields near Clerkenwell, and a good many of them did so. When, however, they reached that open space they found a band of trained men 'by whom the whole force of madmen was surrounded and hemmed in'. When Walworth appeared with Wat Tyler's severed head on a lance the rebels realized that the game was up. By nightfall not one of them remained within the walls of London.

One of Richard's first **actions** was to knight William

Walworth, together with three other worthy merchants, Nicholas Brembre, John Philpot and Robert Launde. When Walworth protested modestly that he was 'only a fishmonger' the King replied by clapping on his head a light steel helmet of the kind usually worn by knights in the field. Grants of land went with these knighthoods, the first ever bestowed upon any London merchant.

The Fishmongers' Company still preserves an ancient weapon said to be the one with which Walworth slew Wat Tyler; but the blade in the top left-hand corner of the City Arms is not, as many people believe, the dagger of that doughty Mayor; it is the sword of St. Paul. The motto, *Domine dirige nos*, means 'God guide us.'

The Fishmongers were proud of William Walworth, and rightly so; but the Grocers must have been equally proud of John Philpot. When in 1377 John of Gaunt threatened the ancient liberties of London Philpot spoke out boldly in their defence; and when in the same year the French pounced upon Hastings and the Isle of Wight and a Scottish pirate, John Mercer, began to prey upon the Channel shipping, Philpot fitted out a small squadron of vessels with a force of one thousand armed men, pursued the pirate, and captured his prizes, among which were fifteen Spanish merchantmen. In 1378 this doughty and far-sighted grocer bore the cost of one of the two stone towers erected below the Bridge to protect London from a possible attack by the French—an attack which never came.

At that time the name of 'Grocer' was comparatively new. It was a dull name, meaning merely a man who dealt in merchandise 'by the gross'. Before 1345 the Company had been known as the Pepperers and Spicers, a much more picturesque title, especially if we remember at what peril the peppers and the spices were brought overseas from the East.

CHAPTER IV

Strife and Splendour

THE Londoners, who had loved the Black Prince well, looked at first with great favour upon his fair-faced young son. They also lent money to him, holding as security many objects of great value and beauty, of which the lists, though not the things, remain. For example, a scarlet hood embroidered with rubies, a coat of cloth-of-gold buttoned with bells of gold, a doublet of tawny satin embroidered with pearls, three brooches in the form of white harts (the royal badge) set with rubies, one Spanish saddle set with precious stones.

Better still did they love his first wife, the gentle Anne of Bohemia. When she came to London as a bride the Mayor and the City Guilds rode out to meet her in great state. A decree had gone forth that they should all wear a plain black and crimson livery, but the Goldsmiths willed it otherwise. They adorned the black cloth with knots of gold and silk, and the crimson cloth with stripes and trefoils of silver.

On one occasion Anne interceded with the King when he was unreasonably annoyed with the citizens. It befell that one of the Bishop of Salisbury's men-servants snatched a loaf out of the basket of a baker's boy who was passing by the Bishop's great house in the Strand, whereupon a mob of unruly people, mostly young apprentices, surged round the house, making much noise but doing little harm. The Bishop himself was with the King at Windsor when he received an account of this riot so highly-coloured that he rushed into the royal presence with loud complaints against these violent ruffians. Richard, not pausing to enquire into the circumstances, behaved quite as impetuously as anybody concerned. He withdrew London's ancient right to elect her own Mayor, he removed from Westminster Hall to the City of York all records of suits and pleas connected with London, and he appointed a *Custos* to rule in the place of the Mayor.

In great dismay the City appealed to two people whom they knew to be able and hoped to be ready to help them— their Bishop and King Richard's Queen. Thanks to their pleading, the King relented, and declared that if four hundred of the principal citizens would come to Sheen Common, near his favourite country palace, and beg his pardon, it would be granted. They came, wearing their long livery-gowns all of one colour; they submitted themselves to him 'in the most lowly wise'; and they besought him 'to take so great peyne upon him' as to ride through London and see for himself how loyal and obedient the citizens were.

To this he agreed: and when in due course he rode across London Bridge from the Surrey side, he found two rich gifts waiting for him—a pair of fine horses in trappings of cloth of gold. Better things still were in store. In Cheapside the houses were hung with tapestry, the people shouted joy-fully 'King Richard, King Richard!' and a child dressed as an angel and standing on a decorated platform bent down to set upon his head, as he rode by, a crown of gold garnished with gems and pearls. Next day the Mayor and other citizens went to Westminster and begged him to accept two golden bowls each containing two thousand gold nobles:[1] and on the morrow the King kindly granted them a confirmation of all their ancient rights and privileges. London was grateful also to her Bishop, Robert Braybrooke. For many years after his death the Mayor and Aldermen would go

---

[1] A noble was a gold coin worth roughly 6s. 8d.

upon certain saints' days to his grave in St. Paul's to pray for his soul.

Some patches in Richard's reign were good and many were gorgeous and gay; but at the end there was nothing but black. Partly owing to the plotting of his cousin, John of Gaunt's exiled son, Henry Bolingbroke, Earl of Derby, and partly owing to his own vanity and waywardness, the once well-loved King had as great a fall as Humpty Dumpty. When he banished his cousin and set at naught the advice of his counsellors and the wishes of his Parliament, he fondly thought that his troubles were at an end, whereas they were only beginning. We think of him mostly as a fool and a failure: yet it should not be forgotten that for eight years he ruled wisely and well, or that during those years London grew in beauty and prosperity.

In 1399 died John of Gaunt. The Savoy being still a ruin, the place of the old man's death was the Bishop of Ely's house in Holborn. In his Will he left instructions that round his tomb in St. Paul's ten tapers should be kindled, to signify the Ten Commandments, all of which he declared that he had broken.

The downfall of Richard the Second, the mystery of his death, and the seizure of the crown by Bolingbroke belong to the history of England rather than to the story of London, but it was in London that some of the last scenes of the tragedy were played out.

Richard was in Ireland when he heard that his kinsman had landed in Yorkshire and was marching on London. He himself landed in Wales, and made some attempt to raise troops and man fortresses, but all in vain. He was betrayed by one of Bolingbroke's supporters, and when the cousins met within the rugged walls of Flint Castle Bolingbroke's first words were to ask if Richard had breakfasted yet. 'No,' returned the King, in some surprise, 'Why do you

ask?' 'Because,' retorted Bolingbroke, 'you have a long way
to ride. You must come to London with me.'

So to London they came. The gates were flung wide,
the citizens poured into the streets to welcome the man so
soon to be crowned King as Henry the Fourth. No one
seems to have spared a pitiful glance to his captive, once the
darling of their hearts.

As soon as Richard was safely housed in the Tower Henry
went to St. Paul's to pray beside the tomb of John of Gaunt
his father, where the ten tapers were flickering and the
priests were chanting, and the shrines of St. Mellitus and St.
Enkenwald glimmered silver and golden in the shadows.

Nobody can tell what was in the mind of the fallen King
when he yielded up his crown, but it is said that he did it
gently and—as it seemed—not unwillingly. Like Charles
the First of England and Nicholas the Second of Russia, he
shone in adversity as he had never shone in his vanished
splendour. While preparations for Henry's coronation went
ahead, Richard, condemned to lifelong captivity, was
secretly removed to an unknown destination in the north.

Henry the Fourth rode to his crowning on his cousin's
favourite horse, a proud and beautiful roan named 'Barbary'.
When the Londoners acclaimed him he bent low over
Barbary's glossy neck saying 'I thank you, countrymen!'

Presently questions began to be asked as to the where-
abouts of the deposed King. His father-in-law, the King of
France, showed an awkward curiosity, and the citizens of
London also became inquisitive. Some, but not all, of their
questions were answered when a solemn procession moved
slowly southward from Pontefract and through the City to
St. Paul's. In the midst was a black-draped bier drawn by a
black-draped horse, and on that bier lay a dead man wasted
and wan, with hollow cheeks and stiffly folded hands. On
his head was a circlet of gold. Three heralds bearing the

royal shields of England walked on either side; steel-capped
men-at-arms and cowled monks brought up the rear; and
so they came to London and passed through the silent
crowds to the cathedral. During the two days that he lay in
state hundreds of people came to peer into his haggard face.
They knew then that Richard was dead; but how he died
no one knew then and no one knows for certain now.

Funeral Procession of Richard the Second

'*They bore him barefaced on his bier*'

From an illuminated Manuscript of Froissart's Chronicle. British Museum

For one reason if for no other this unhappy King deserves
to be remembered by Londoners. It was he who in June,
1397, issued a mandate declaring that as he wished to provide
for 'the wise governance and happy rule of the City' he had
with the assent and advice of his Council appointed to the
office of Mayor 'his well-beloved Richard Whittington'.
This remarkable citizen was re-elected in 1406 and again in
1409—the only Mayor of London to be a hero in nursery
legend and in pantomime.

Few Londoners have been more famous; yet he was not a Londoner born. He came from Pauntley, in what was then the distant county of Gloucestershire, but when he came or to whom he was bound apprentice is not known. He was still a comparatively young man when his name began to appear as a subscriber of considerable sums to City loans; later, he became a member of one of the most powerful and wealthy of the City Companies, that of the Mercers.

What of his celebrated cat, also a favourite pantomime personage? The old story ran that he took it with him on a journey to Morocco, where the clever animal won rich rewards for its master by ridding the Sultan's Palace of mice: but there were old stories very like this long before his time and in more lands than one. Was the famous cat really a 'Catt', a type of merchant ship in which Whittington may have made his first lucky venture? Nobody knows. Yet it is not many years since a stone figure of a boy holding an unmistakable cat was discovered in the foundations of a house built in Gloucester by Whittington's nephew.

This 'Flower of Merchants' lent large sums both to Henry the Fourth and Henry the Fifth. He furnished rich silken stuffs for the trousseaux of the Princesses Blanche and Philippa, and money supplied by him helped to pay and equip the English archers at Agincourt. Not until after his death did it become known that he remembered and pitied Richard the Second, that brilliant butterfly, whose name appears among the short list of people for whose souls prayers were to be said daily by the thirteen aged poor men in his almshouse on Highgate Hill. Whittington planned his good deeds carefully. He founded chapels, almshouses and libraries, helped to repair St. Bartholomew's Hospital, contributed to the restoration of Guildhall, and set up bosses in the London streets so that the inhabitants might be able to obtain water as pure as the conditions of the time allowed.

Londoners may have felt a little uneasy when Henry the Fourth died. Rumour said that his son, the Prince of Wales, was a mere madcap. They soon learned how little cause they had for fear.

In March, 1415, the young King summoned to the Tower Thomas Fauconer, the Mayor, together with the Aldermen and certain leading citizens, that he might inform them of his intention 'with a small army to visit the parts beyond the sea', so that he might re-conquer 'the lands pertaining to his heritage'—namely the realm of France. He also announced that he would send 'certain lords of his Council' to treat with the City 'as to promoting the business aforesaid', or, in other words, to raise a loan. The City scribe did not forget to record that these lords agreed that the Mayor should sit between the Archbishop of Canterbury and the Bishop of Winchester, a place of great honour.

Three months later London lent the King 10,000 marks, receiving as security a magnificent jewelled collar weighing fifty-six ounces and enclosed in a leather case sealed with the arms of the royal treasurer, Richard, Bishop of Norwich. Most of the great officers of the realm were churchmen. Merchants and craftsmen who could not write kept accounts by making notches on what were called 'tally sticks'. It was the accidental igniting of a large accumulation of these sticks, old, brittle and dry, which started the fire that destroyed the Houses of Parliament in 1834.

The 'New Work' at the Guildhall was now in progress though not yet completed. The necessary funds were being raised in various ways. Every barber who shaved a customer, or cut his hair, or allowed his wife, son, daughter, apprentice or servant to do so, on the Sabbath day was fined 6s. 8d. of which 5s. went towards the New Work and 1s. to the Master of the Barbers' Company. This gives us a quaint picture of a fifteenth-century barber's shop, in which the whole family might be seen at work together when business was brisk.

Before setting sail for France in his ship, the *Trinity Royal*, the King took a cordial farewell of his capital city. Much of the City's loan must have gone towards the adornment of the English fleet, which made a magnificent spectacle with its gilded figure-heads, its sails painted with a hundred

Ships of the Early Fifteenth Century

'Fairy Tale vessels'

From an illuminated Manuscript. British Museum

different devices, its many-coloured standards and streamers, its square banners bearing designs of golden leopards, white ostrich feathers, or the arms of England and St. George. Many Londoners sailed in those fairy-tale vessels, and many fought valiantly in the campaign that followed.

Presently word came of the capture of Harfleur. This Norman seaport was, it seemed, to be occupied permanently by Londoners and other good English folk. The King was marching on Calais and hoped to reach that place about October 16. The Mayor accordingly despatched a messenger thither with a sum of £100 for the use of the Army upon its arrival, and supplies for the sick and wounded were also on their way. But time passed, and no news came, and frightening rumours of defeat and disaster began to circulate. It was even said that the King had fallen.

On October 29 the newly-elected Mayor, Nicholas Wolton (unkindly nicknamed 'Nick the Witless'), having been duly sworn in, was to ride to Westminster to be formally received by the Barons of the Exchequer as representing the absent King; but early that morning, before the merchants had unbarred their shutters, a royal herald came spurring into London bearing the glorious news of Agincourt. The mood of the City changed in a flash. Bells rang out, the *Te Deum* was chanted in every parish church, huge crowds thronged into St. Paul's to hear Henry Beaufort, Bishop of Winchester,[1] read aloud the official announcement of the victory. In their excitement the Mayor and the citizens decided to do what they had never done before— that is, to proceed *on foot* 'like pilgrims' to Westminster, there to give thanks before the shrine of the 'glorious Confessor', St. Edward. The City scribe is careful to set down that these Londoners had gone on foot instead of on horseback because of the great relief and joy which followed those days of uncertainty and dismay: but their horses must have reached Westminster in time to be mounted and ridden back to London, for it was upon horseback that they returned after the thanksgiving service.

When the King reached Blackheath on his way to London one November day in 1415, the City surpassed herself in the splendour of the welcome she gave him. To meet him rode the Mayor and Aldermen and between 15,000 and 20,000 craftsmen, clad in red and white. When he had greeted them, they formed a procession, and, with great noise of trumpets, escorted him to St. Paul's, by way of Southwark, London

---

[1] John of Gaunt's son.

Bridge, Cornhill and Cheapside. The clergy welcomed him with a Latin chant beginning

Hail! Flower of England, pure soldier of Christ!

As the many-coloured cavalcade crossed the Bridge the King exclaimed loudly 'Hail to the royal city! Christ keep her from sorrow and care!'

A great effort had been made to cleanse the streets, which were strewn with sand or straw. Boughs of evergreen and rich tapestries adorned the houses. Mock towers stood by the way, surmounted by figures of giants and giantesses, saints and angels. From a roof-top a choir of boys, white-robed, white-winged, golden-wigged, sang, to the accompaniment of organs, an anthem beginning 'Welcome, Sovereign Lord!' The cavalcade took five hours to reach Westminster. In the centre rode the King himself, a slender figure clad in a simple purple cloak, an expression of seriousness, almost sternness, on his long, narrow face. His desire that all the honour should be paid to God and none to himself was respected, more or less: but the people were disappointed when he declined to have borne through the streets the battered armour and the dinted helmet which he had worn in battle.

Many charade-like pageants slowed down the progress, but none can have been more pleasing than that enacted by a group of greybeards in crimson turbans who released a flock of sparrows and other small birds. Surely the King's grave looks relaxed into a smile when the little creatures fluttered round him and even perched on his shoulder!

Six years later London had another opportunity to show what she could do, and royally she rose to it. This was when Henry's French bride, the Princess Catherine, made her state entry. Giants bowed before her, lions rolled their eyes at her, angels sang to her. Green boughs strewed the streets, and members of the City companies escorted her on horse-back, while bells rang, trumpets blew, and the admiring people cheered.

At her coronation banquet in Westminster Hall two days later the Mayor, Aldermen and principal citizens of London occupied a table 'next unto the cupboorde'—the sideboard upon which great vessels of gold and silver-gilt were set forth.

Armour and Saddle of Henry the Fifth from his Tomb at Westminster

Carried through London at his funeral

Soon after this the King was called back to France, where death and disaster had overtaken his younger brother, the Duke of Clarence, in the battle of Baugé. London never saw again her stern and heroic Henry. There was great rejoicing when, in the month of December, the news came that a prince had been born at Windsor, the future Henry the Sixth: but only nine months later joy was turned to mourning by the death of Henry the Fifth.

His funeral procession moved slowly through France to Calais and thence by sea to Dover. Four powerful horses drew the black-draped car on which lay a rather startling figure, larger than life-size, moulded out of a substance known as *cuir-bouilli* or boiled leather, the face as far as might be resembling the well-known features of the dead King. Royal robes draped it, a royal crown was set upon its head and a royal sceptre in the rigid right hand.

When the cavalcade reached Blackheath the Mayor and the Aldermen were there, dressed in deepest black, to escort the coffin to St. Paul's, where it lay that night. Next day they went forth again, as the great car with its impressive effigy rolled towards Westminster, under its proud canopy of cloth of gold.

'And', says a chronicler of that time, 'in the same year almost all the laurel-trees in England withered away.'

The little King Henry the Sixth was only four years old when his Uncle, Humphrey, Duke of Gloucester, decided that he should attend a solemn public service in St. Paul's. He was 'led upon his feet' to the choir and thence carried to a chair near the High Altar. Afterwards he was lifted on to a richly-caparisoned horse and conducted along Cheapside, 'looking gravely upon the people', who for their part looked lovingly upon him.

Surprising events in France caused the little boy's uncle to hurry on his crowning. In 1429 word came that a young girl from Lorraine, clad in white armour and bearing a painted banner in her hand, had raised the siege of Orleans and entered the city in triumph, in spite of all that the English could do to keep her out. Three months later Charles the Seventh, little Henry's uncle, was crowned King of France in the cathedral at Rheims. The English were amazed. Surely this Joan of Arc must be a witch, inspired by Satan. Never could God work a miracle on behalf of the French. Henry the Sixth must be crowned King of France in Paris without delay. But of course the coronation at Westminster must come first. Therefore on November 6th, 1429, 'a clear and bright day', the pale, solemn child was conducted with all the traditional pomp from the Tower to the Abbey. The

Mayor of London, carrying the crystal sceptre, was among those who saw with what immense gravity the King went through the long-drawn-out and complicated ceremonial; he acted as Butler at the banquet in Westminster Hall, and received a gold cup and ewer as his reward.

The Londoners, little foreseeing the time when the greater part of Christendom would revere her as a Saint, rejoiced heartily when they heard of the trial and execution of Joan of Arc at Rouen in May, 1431. They sent 10,000 crowns to the Duke of Bedford's troops to encourage them in their long and—as it turned out—hopeless struggle against the French.

During the minority of young Henry the City was disturbed and perplexed by the constant disagreements between the uncles of the King. On the whole the citizens were inclined to side with Humphrey, Duke of Gloucester, who, during the absence of John, Duke of Bedford, in France, acted as Protector of England. Humphrey had, after all, fought at Agincourt and might have perished there had not his brother the King spurred to his rescue. He lived on Thames-side, at Baynard's Castle, the one-time home of Robert Fitz-Walter, leader of the Magna Carta Barons; he was affable, good-looking and gay. They did not realize that he was also both greedy and unscrupulous. They certainly liked him better than they did Henry Beaufort, Bishop of Winchester, a prelate always anxious to have every finger in every pie.

One autumn evening in the year 1425 the Duke summoned the Mayor and the Aldermen to his castle and warned them to watch well over the City that night, especially the Bridge. The Bishop's palace was at Southwark, and early next morning it became known that an alarming number of his men, knights, squires and archers had appeared there, pulled up the chains between the posts and established themselves in the gatehouse. In the space of an hour every shop in London was shuttered while the citizens hurried to bar and man the gates at their own end of the Bridge. It was an ugly situation, but the Archbishop of Canterbury intervened, and no one prevented him from riding to and fro no less than eight times between the Duke and the Bishop, so that finally the Mayor and Aldermen were able to prevail upon the people to disperse to their homes. When John of Bedford heard of these incidents, he came over from France to restore order, and received with no outward signs of gratitude a present of 1,000 marks from the City of London.

Neither the Londoners nor Beaufort bore any grudge. When he was made a Cardinal the Mayor and Aldermen welcomed him 'royally and worthily', and when he came to die he bequeathed £4,000 to relieve the sufferings of the poor folk in the prisons of London.

The City did not, however, approve of his policy of appeasement with France, and agreed with Duke Humphrey that the surrender of the English possessions in Anjou and Maine was too high a price to pay for the hand in marriage of the proud, penniless French Princess, Margaret of Anjou. Particularly did the citizens dislike the Cardinal's upstart henchman, William de la Pole, Earl of Suffolk, who went to France to bring the bride home. None the less, they turned out as in duty bound to welcome her, the Mayor and Aldermen in scarlet, the City Companies in blue, and they escorted to the Tower of London not only the young Queen but the seventeen chariots containing the ladies of her household, who must have looked like so many gay butterflies in their fashionable headdresses winged with white lawn.

Five years earlier the Mayor, Aldermen and Sheriffs had been called upon to take part in a very different procession. Duke Humphrey's second wife, Eleanor Cobham, was accused and found guilty of trying by means of magic, and with the aid of witches and wizards, to shorten the King's life so that her husband might reign in his stead. They were said to have made a wax image of Henry and to have prayed, while they held it over a slow fire, that as the wax melted his strength might melt away. The witch who had taken part in the performance was burned alive at Smithfield; two other accomplices died, one mysteriously in the Tower and one by hanging at Tyburn; and the Duchess was condemned to do public penance through the streets of London, bareheaded, barefoot, clad in a long white sheet and carrying a lighted taper in her hand. This penance she did three times; once she went to St. Paul's, once to Christ Church, Aldgate, and once to St. Michael-on-Cornhill. It was on the third occasion that the Mayor, Aldermen and Sheriffs walked solemnly behind her.

One by one the leading figures in the play vanished from the scene. Duke Humphrey died—or, perhaps, was murdered —at Bury St. Edmund's in February, 1447; Cardinal Beaufort departed this life at Winchester only six weeks later; and in 1450 William de la Pole, Duke of Suffolk, greediest of all the shamelessly greedy courtiers, having been impeached by Parliament and banished by the King, was seized by his enemies on a ship off Dover and cruelly beheaded with a rusty sword.

Henry, urged on by Margaret, resolved to punish the people of the whole county of Kent for the murder of de la Pole because the deed was done near the Kentish coast; and he thereby kindled a fire which spread as far as London and might well have destroyed the City.

In June, 1450, Londoners were startled to hear that an army of between thirty and forty thousand rebels, led by an Irishman named Jack Cade, was marching on the City. Most of the rebels were Kentish folk, but they were joined by others from Sussex and elsewhere, and they had friends within the walls of London. At first nothing very dreadful happened. Cade sent to the King a document setting forth the complaints of the people of Kent, and when he received a cautious reply he followed this up with a more peremptory manifesto entitled 'The Requests of the Captain of the Great Assembly in Kent'. He demanded that the King should dismiss all his false counsellors, live within his income, and punish the traitors who had caused the death of 'that nota-bylle and famos prynce the Duke of Gloceter'. He also intimated his desire that the King's kinsman, Richard, Duke of York, with other noble princes and peers, should be recalled to his Council. The fact that Cade was an Irishman and that the Duke of York was at that time an exile in Ireland suggests that the rebellion was the first move in a Yorkist plot to overthrow the line of Lancaster, as represented by Henry the Sixth, and set up instead a new royal dynasty tracing its descent from Edmund, Duke of York, fifth son of Edward the Third.

Certain especially hated courtiers were named, among them Lord Saye, Great Treasurer of England, but in the meantime the King had collected a sufficient force of armed men to quell (as it was believed) this Kentish rising. An impressive force rode through the streets of London and over London Bridge. The King himself, in full armour, went with them for part of the way, and with him went ten thousand nobles, knights and men at arms, under the command of Sir Humphrey Stafford, seeming, as an eye-witness wrote, 'redy to go to batayle into any lande in Christyndom'.

The Londoners breathed freely again. But presently word came that this gorgeous host had been defeated by Jack Cade at Sevenoaks and that Sir Humphrey Stafford had been slain when fleeing from the field; and this bad news was soon afterwards followed by the return of the rebel army to Blackheath in full force and high spirits.

Panic appears to have seized both the City and the Court. Lord Scales was left with a thousand men to defend the Tower, but the disheartened royal army was disbanded and the King himself withdrew hastily to Kenilworth.

Cade meanwhile occupied Southwark and demanded to be admitted to the City of London. He swaggered about in the gold-studded armour of poor Sir Humphrey Stafford, and, abandoning the homely name of 'Cade', declared himself to be a member of the noble house of Mortimer and related to the Duke of York.

With the King far away, the royal forces scattered, and Lord Scales shut up in the Tower with his thousand men, it is hardly surprising that the Mayor and Aldermen in Council decided to offer no resistance to the self-styled 'John Mortimer'. It was even reported that Richard Philip, a grocer, and Thomas Gosper, a spurrier, unbarred the Bridge gates to let him in. Cade severed the ropes of the drawbridge as he rode by, so that no one could raise it and thus cut him off from his base at Southwark, to which he returned every night during the strange and evil days which followed. The 'Captain' himself took up his quarters in the best tavern there, at the sign of the White Hart.

According to an ancient superstition no one was lord of London who had not touched London Stone.[1] Cade accordingly struck that venerable relic with his sword, and shouted 'Now Mortimer is lord of London!'

His next step was to compel the Mayor and Aldermen to try Lord Saye in Guildhall on a charge of high treason. It was a mockery of a trial, for according to law a man could be tried only by his equals in rank, but Saye had no friends in the City nor did he deserve to have any. They hauled him out to Cheapside, hacked off his head, and afterwards stuck it on a pole over the Bridge.

[1] This ancient relic is still to be seen near Cannon Street station.

At first Cade was able to control his followers fairly well, but before long they began to plunder the houses of the richer citizens and to lay violent hands upon anyone who resisted them. One eye-witness notes some of the property which they stole from the house and shop of an Alderman named Philip Malpas—silver and gold, wood and tin, woollen stuffs, feather-beds, linen, and such rich arras-cloths as were hung upon walls.

Whatever sympathy the citizens may have felt with the wrongs of the people of Kent, however little they may have approved of the doings of some of the royal Counsellors, they had no sympathy with robbery and violence. The Mayor contrived to send a messenger to 'goode olde Lorde Scales' in the Tower, with the result that his lordship, aided by Matthew Gough, a veteran of the French wars, took command of the City Bands and led them against Cade and his ruffians. For ten hours a desperate battle raged on London Bridge. Cade seems to have lost his head. One of his wild deeds was to break open the prisons of the King's Bench and the Marshalsea and set all the prisoners free; but he showed some presence of mind when he set fire to the drawbridge on the Southwark side and thereby prevented the victorious Londoners from purusing him when he withdrew his army in that direction.

An attempt was later made to trick him into surrender by the offer of free pardon under the great seal, but in the end he realized that all was lost. His followers were quarrelling over their booty; nothing more was to be expected in the way of help or sympathy from the all-powerful City of London: and when a reward of £1,000 was offered for his capture, alive or dead, he fled on horseback into Sussex.

The reward was won by the Sheriff of that pleasant county, Alexander Iden, who found Cade skulking in his garden, and, after a short, sharp fight, dispatched him.

The cart carrying Cade's body to London halted at the White Hart, Southwark, so that the landlady might identify the dead man as the same who had lodged there 'in his previous time of misrule'. Within the walls of the King's Bench his head was struck off; and presently the Londoners saw it stuck up on a pole over the Bridge where they had fought so doughtily against him and his ruffianly rabble.

CHAPTER V

London and the Two Roses

THANKS to a poet of the fifteenth century it is possible to imagine how London would impress a simple fellow up for the first time from the country. He was deafened by the cries of the street sellers bawling their wares —fresh cherries, boiled ribs of beef, and 'many a pie'; he was surprised when the long-robed lawyers in Westminster Hall refused to give him free advice; and he was indignant when he recognized exposed for sale on a stall in the City his own good grey hood stolen that same morning at Westminster. 'I knew it,' he says, 'as well as I know my creed.'

Whether he went along the Strand or along the Thames he must have passed by the Temple, now no longer the headquarters of the Knights Templar, whose order had been suppressed by the Pope in the year 1312. Their famous circular church was gutted by incendiaries in World War II; but the City Solicitor still pays rent for a forge set up on their tilting-ground in the year 1230. This is a 'token rent' consisting of six horse-shoes and sixty-one nails. The same shoes and nails have been handed over every year for more than four centuries.

Another order of military monks, the Hospitallers, occupied the Temple for a time, but in the reign of Edward the Second the lawyers took possession of the place which their successors have held ever since. Woven in flags or wrought in iron the device of the long-vanished Templars is still to be seen—a flying horse. In its early days, when they

had been vowed to poverty, they bore a different device—
two men riding economically on one horse; but as they grew
wealthy and proud the two men changed somehow into two
wings.

The King's Bench in the Fifteenth Century

*Judges in robes and coifs, sergeants-at-law in parti-coloured gowns, and,
in the foreground, six shackled prisoners 'at the bar'*

From a Legal Treatise of the Period

When one of these legal 'Templars' was appointed a
Sergeant-at-Law half of his robe would thenceforth be of
plain stuff, and half of striped silk. The robe of a Judge was

scarlet trimmed with fur, and both he and the barristers appearing before him wore tight-fitting white linen hoods called 'coifs'. The little circular patch of white silk on the top of a modern Judge's wig is a visible relic of the 'coif' and his dignified robes have altered little since the days of the later Plantagenets.

The Knights Templar, and after them the lawyers, had a pleasant garden. There is one on the same spot to this day. According to Shakespeare in the *First Part of King Henry the Sixth* it was in this garden that a group of Yorkist and Lancastrian leaders each gathered either a white rose or a red to proclaim his allegiance: but a white rose was the badge of York and a red rose the badge of Lancaster long before the Wars of the Roses began.

Though no battle in those Wars was fought nearer to London than Barnet, the City and the citizens took part in several of the episodes which led up to the triumph of the White Rose in the person of Edward the Fourth. At first their sympathies veered towards the Red Rose; but they disliked the masterful Queen and her friend and counsellor, the Duke of Somerset, nor did they forget that her marriage treaty had involved a considerable loss of English territory in France. Presently the scales dipped in favour of Richard of York, who could claim double descent from Edward the Third and was the father of several tall sons.

The chief concern of the City was naturally trade. Peace at home, good markets abroad, a settled government and no excessive taxes—it did not matter much whether the King's name were Ned, or Harry, or Dick, so long as he gave to Londoners what they needed most and liked best. For some time they obtained none of these things from either side. Fortune inclined now one way and now another. No less than three times the cathedral of St. Paul was the scene of a solemn public service of reconciliation, when mortal foes knelt side by side to receive the sacrament and then came forth hand in hand before the wondering gaze of the people.

In January, 1458, a council was summoned to meet in London. The Duke of York, the Earl of Salisbury, and his son, the Earl of Warwick, appeared before the gates with a considerable force of retainers, but there was no reluctance to let them enter the City and take up their abode in their respective palaces. It is true that the Mayor, at the head of 5,000 armed citizens, patrolled the streets to keep the peace, but as the Lancastrians were compelled to lodge outside the walls this task was not so difficult as it might have been.

The Red Rose partisans met at the monastery of the Carmelites, the White Friars, while the White Rose party met at the headquarters of the Dominicans, the Black Friars. The noble buildings where they gathered have vanished long since, but the names 'Carmelite', 'Whitefriars' and 'Blackfriars' have survived, and are seen and heard every day in the postal district E.C.4.

The terms dictated by King Henry reflected his saintly, unpractical character. Nobody was to be called a traitor. Everybody was to forgive everybody else. And the bells of London rang out to celebrate an agreement which seemed to promise so well.

Only a month later word came to London that the Earl of Warwick, cruising in the English Channel, had attacked a large fleet of ships laden with merchandise from Lübeck and had captured five of them, which he took to Calais as prizes. These ships belonged to the group of German cities known as the Hanseatic League, whose merchants had been encouraged by Henry the Third and Edward the First to settle and trade in London, where they had had headquarters ever since 1250.[1] Little though the Londoners liked these—

[1] They were not formally expelled till 1597–8 when Elizabeth the First drove them out.

or any other—foreigners, security of commerce was as necessary to them as to any other trading community; they had not much to say in defence of Warwick when, at the request of the League, he was summoned to appear before the Royal Council and answer for his piratical proceedings.

The Earl of Warwick receiving the gift of a Book

Londoners knew him well by sight during his lifetime: after his death in battle at Barnet they saw his dead body, stripped of all its armour, lying forlorn in St. Paul's

From an illuminated Manuscript in the British Museum

Brawls followed, and Warwick, believing, or pretending to believe, that his life was in danger, fled to his father, the Earl of Salisbury, in Yorkshire, and the stage was set for the next act of these bitter wars.

In the summer of 1460 Warwick was back again, and soon word came to London that Henry had been defeated and captured at Northampton. Presently he was paraded through the streets, meek and unresisting, Warwick riding bare-

headed before him, carrying the great sword of state. After
much argument it was agreed that he should be King for
life, but that York and his eldest son should stand next in
the line of succession, the claims of young Edward, Prince
of Wales, being set aside. This was the third and last of the
processions to St. Paul's, but on this occasion Queen Margaret
took no part in it. She was far away in the north at the head
of an army of rough peasants to whom she held out the promise of plundering the richest city in the world—London.

That City was stunned when news came of the Yorkist
disaster at Wakefield. Worse still, Margaret was marching
southward as fiercely bent upon revenge as her followers
were eager for booty.

Edward, Earl of March had become, upon the death of
his father at Wakefield, the natural leader of the White Rose.
News of his doings came slowly to London, for he was far
away in the West, rallying his friends about him, but when
it did come it put new heart into those who had nothing but
loathing for Margaret and little but compassion for Henry.
This tall, red-haired, eighteen-year-old Plantagenet had won
the battle of Mortimer's Cross and was believed to be marching on the capital. Margaret, fresh from her last victory in
the second battle of St. Albans, was likewise bound for
London, with her husband whom she had rescued from
captivity. In his name as well as in her own she promised
that her 'northerners' should remain outside the walls, but
at the same time she demanded immediate supplies for that
hungry host.

It must have been difficult for the Mayor and Aldermen
to know what to do. In the end they ordered some wagons
to be loaded up with supplies, but citizens, who had other
ideas, overturned these wagons as they creaked along
Cripplegate and shared the contents among themselves.

When, shortly afterwards, 400 Lancastrian horsemen

plundered some outlying districts North of the City, London had had enough. The gates flew open at the approach of Edward of York, the people poured into the streets to greet him, and they joined in a shout of 'Yea, Yea' which made the roof of Westminster Hall ring when the handsome young Plantagenet, seated on a golden chair of state, asked if they would have him for their King.

Edward's victory at Towton in March was followed by his Coronation at Westminster in June. Four years later the Londoners had another glimpse of Henry the Sixth, when he was paraded through the streets on his way to the Tower. For another five years he was kept there, and as the citizens looked across the moat at the grim grey walls they must often have wondered how the royal prisoner was faring, he whose heroic father their own fathers had acclaimed so loudly on his return from Agincourt.

For a time London liked her young King Edward the Fourth very well. It was hoped that by wedding the daughter of some great foreign prince he might open up new markets abroad, and he did indeed marry his sister Margaret to Charles, Duke of Burgundy: but merchants are seldom romantically-minded, and his own marriage to a beautiful widow, Elizabeth Woodville pleased them of the City not at all, especially when the new Queen's father and brother and her sons by her first husband, Sir John Gray, rose rapidly in royal favour. It looked like being the story of the Beauforts over again.

None the less the people crowded to Smithfield one day in 1467 to see her brother Anthony, Earl Rivers, jousting on horseback and on foot against Antoine of Burgundy, one of the most renowned jousters of the time.

A splendid figure must Rivers have made, clad in glittering steel and mounted on a horse trapped with cloth of silver bearing a St. George's cross in crimson velvet; the golden fringe was six inches deep. The Burgundian's horse had housings of crimson velvet, adorned with bells of silver and gold. Each animal had a steel *chamfron*, or head-protector, with a spike in the centre, and there was a good deal of laughter when the horse of the visitor, by some extraordinary chance, stunned itself by running its head against the high pommel of the Englishman's saddle. On foot the two warriors fought lustily with battle-axes and long daggers, but the King, perhaps anxious for personal and political reasons that neither should be seriously hurt, soon cast down his bâton as a signal that the fight should stop.

Burgundians who came over to see the sight were much impressed by the good looks and unusual height of the King, but even more by the fact that in the very presence of the sovereign the great, pearl-handled City sword was carried upright and unsheathed before the Mayor. This sword is still seen by guests at the Lord Mayor's banquet every year.

Two years later London was humming with rumours. The King had fallen out with his brother, George, Duke of Clarence, and with his powerful supporter, the Earl of Warwick, both of whom were ambitious and not over-trustworthy, and both of whom hated the Woodvilles and the Grays. Then came the startling news that they had joined hands against the King and defeated him near Banbury. By the end of 1470 the gay and gallant Edward had fled to the court of his brother-in-law, the Duke of Burgundy, and Warwick was offering to exchange the White Rose for the Red if Queen Margaret would agree to a match between her son, the Prince of Wales, and his daughter Anne. His other daughter, Isabel, was married to Clarence.

Then once more the Londoners saw King Henry when, pale from his long imprisonment, he was led on horseback through the streets, gentle and unresisting, his crown upon his meek grey head.

Hardly had the City accepted this unexpected event than word came from the coast of Suffolk which altered everything. Edward, with a small force of Burgundians, had landed there, a reasonable, conciliatory Edward, quite ready to swear allegiance to Henry, if only he might have restored to him the domains and possessions of his late father, the Duke of York. Warwick, he said, was the real enemy of peace. If once that stirrer-up of trouble were got rid of, all strife would soon be at an end.

It seemed too good to be true that Edward was willing to give up his claims to the crown. It *was* too good to be true. Recruits flocked to his banner as he marched through Nottinghamshire and Warwickshire towards London. Clarence hastily changed sides, and handed out white rose badges to his followers whom he had previously decked with red ones.

And now for the last time Henry was hoisted on to his horse and made to ride slowly through London, in the hope that the old loyalty of the people might be revived. It was too late. As he rode he passed detachments of the City Bands, the well-armed and well-trained militia, marching on their way to join Edward, who had boldly proclaimed himself the sole and rightful lord of the realm. London had had enough of a puppet King, a masterful Queen, and a scheming nobleman who sought to make and unmake Kings for his own advantage. The gates flew open to let Edward in. Though the Wars of the Roses were not yet over, the issue was no longer in doubt.

The next battle was fought at Barnet on a misty April morning in 1471, and it was a Yorkist victory. Warwick nicknamed 'The Kingmaker' died upon the field, and his body, stripped of its rich armour, lay for a time in St. Paul's for all London to look at, a pitiful sight.

Then Queen Margaret, with her son, the Red Rose Prince

of Wales, and her son's bride, the Kingmaker's daughter, Anne, landed at Weymouth in the highest hope, only to be met by the news of the Lancastrian defeat. She was not daunted. She rallied her friends round her for a march on London. Edward was too quick for her. The two armies met near Tewkesbury, at the place where the Avon and the Severn mingle their waters, and there was fought the last battle of the Wars of the Roses. The young Prince of Wales perished, rather mysteriously, during or after the fray, and on the night that King Edward returned in triumph to London King Henry died—also mysteriously—in the Tower. The Yorkists declared that the Lancastrian King's death was caused by 'grief and melancholy', but later, when evil reports began to gather round the name of Richard, Duke of Gloucester, people remembered that he had been within the walls of the Tower when Henry died. Some years ago Henry's tomb at Windsor was opened, and it was then found that the skull had been broken, probably during life, and that the hair was stiff with dried blood. Tradition points to a recess in the White Tower as the spot where he was slain, and there a sheaf of lilies lies every year on his anniversary, a token of remembrance from his College at Eton.

Among the loyal Londoners whom Edward knighted in his hour of triumph was John Crosby, Alderman, woolstapler and Member of Parliament. While the King was absent in the West Country during the spring of the year a certain Thomas Neville, sometimes called 'Fauconberg', decided to make a bold attempt to capture London for the Red Rose. Under Henry the Sixth he had been Vice-Admiral of the English Channel, but finding his occupation gone he turned pirate and gathered round him, as an old historian puts it, 'many Persons of desperate Fortunes'. Marching through Kent at the head of a motley Army, quite in the manner of Wat Tyler and Jack Cade, he pitched his camp at Southwark. He was a better strategist than either Wat or Jack, for he landed some of his men on the north bank of the Thames, east of the City wall, with orders to attack Aldgate and Bishopsgate, while he himself, with the main body, tried to take London Bridge by storm and so break into the City. It was a clever plan, but the valour of the Londoners brought it to naught. The Queen's brother, Earl Rivers, fought side by side with them, and they repulsed

the attack on their gates with such energy that Fauconberg had no choice but to call off his followers and beat a retreat. Foremost among the defenders of Bishopsgate was John Crosby. He had a personal motive for wishing to keep this violent mob out of that quarter, for he was then building for himself in Bishopsgate Street a beautiful house of stone and timber, the highest at that time in London.[1] Such were the merchants of Plantagenet London—dwellers in princely houses, wielders of doughty blades. Crosby's tomb in the Priory Church of St. Helen's shows him wearing the collar of suns and roses which was the reward of the House of York

[1] Crosby Hall was pulled down in 1908 to make way for a railway station, but the stones and the rafters were carefully numbered and have been fitted together again on the river bank at Chelsea.

to its faithful friends, and his suit of plate armour suggests a knight whose proper place was on the battlefield or in the lists instead of at a desk with a quill in his hand.

London can little have guessed when Edward died in April, 1483, how near the old line of the Plantagenets was to being snuffed out, or how soon a new dynasty would possess the throne. The City was the scene of many of the events, some strange, some mysterious, some terrible, which marked the change.

It will be remembered that Warwick the 'King-maker' had married his daughter Isabel to George, the White Rose Duke of Clarence, and then—as the price of his support— had betrothed his daughter Anne to the Red Rose Prince of Wales, thus seeking to make sure that whichever Rose remained longest in bloom his descendants should become royal.

Anne returned to England with her might-have-been mother-in-law, Margaret of Anjou, and was captured after the Yorkist triumph at Tewkesbury. By the death of Warwick at the Battle of Barnet, Isabel and Anne became co-heiresses to his great possessions, which Clarence, then reconciled with his brother, King Edward, wished very much to keep entirely for himself and his Duchess. He was much annoyed when he found that his younger brother, Richard, Duke of Gloucester, was wooing Anne. There is no reason to believe that Anne was ever as reluctant as Shakespeare, following Tudor history-books, makes her out to be at the beginning of his play of *Richard the Third*; nor was Richard the hideous monster of Tudor imagination. Edward had heaped rewards upon the one brother who had been loyal to him all through, so greed of gold cannot have been Gloucester's motive.

Clarence, in his anxiety to prevent this match, actually dressed 'the Lady Anne' in the grey gown and white hood of a maidservant and kept her hidden somewhere in London thus disguised. Gloucester, however, penetrated the disguise and carried her off to sanctuary at St. Martin's le Grand, where she may have rubbed elbows with some very rough and alarming fugitives from justice during the short time that she remained there. No doubt the clergy of the ancient church kept her apart from the other sanctuary-seekers, but it would be a frightening experience.

Edward the Fourth, appealed to by both his brothers, decided in favour of Gloucester, who accordingly married Anne and took her to Middleham Castle in Yorkshire, where their only child, a boy named Edward, was born, and where they were living when Edward the Fourth died. Clarence meanwhile had perished mysteriously in the Tower, drowned, according to some, in a butt of malmsey, a sweet, strong-flavoured red wine of which he was very fond. When Edward the Fourth died his elder son was far away at Ludlow with his uncle, Earl Rivers, and his half-brother Lord John Gray. Rivers was the earliest patron of William Caxton, the first Englishman to set up a printing-press; in many ways he was an interesting man, a thinker and a dreamer as well as a fighter; but the English people felt that if their little King must remain for a few years in the care of a guardian, they would prefer his father's brother, Richard Duke of Gloucester, to be the man.

Events moved rapidly. Rivers and Gray were hastily executed on the rather wild charge that they had plotted against the Duke. Edward the Fifth wept when told that they were both wicked men; but while he was in the Tower waiting for his Coronation he must have found many things to interest him as well as many that were very puzzling. His mother, his five sisters and his brother, Richard, Duke of York, were all in sanctuary at Westminster Abbey. Why should his brother refuse to come forth? Surely not for fear of the kind uncle who was so busy with preparations for the crowning!

Presently the King had a playmate near his own age—his brother, whom the Archbishop of Canterbury had persuaded his mother to give up. But the City wondered when the

Earl Rivers presenting a printed book to Edward the Fourth

Caxton kneels on the left: on the King's right hand are Queen Elizabeth Woodville and the Prince of Wales, afterwards one of the two Princes in the Tower

From an illuminated Manuscript at Lambeth Palace

Coronation date was put off first from May 4th to June 22nd, and then from June 22nd to November 4th. Strange events made tongues wag. At a meeting of the Royal Council, held in the Tower, Gloucester, suddenly, with a pale and agitated face, declared that the Queen, Lord Hastings, and Jane Shore, the wife of a London merchant, had been plotting against him, by magic and otherwise. The accusation crashed like a thunderbolt out of a blue sky, for only a few minutes earlier the Duke was chatting amiably with the Bishop of Ely and asking for a basket of the famous strawberries from his garden at Ely Place, Holborn. Yet the death of Rivers and Gray upon the same charge was fresh in every mind, nor was the penance of Eleanor, Duchess of Gloucester, forgotten.[1]

Soon afterwards a messenger came to Guildhall begging that some of the chief citizens would at once repair to the presence of Gloucester. When, marvelling much, they obeyed, they found him and his kinsman, Henry Stafford, Duke of Buckingham, (another descendant of John of Gaunt) wearing hastily-donned and rusty suits of armour and explaining excitedly that they had only just escaped from a plot to kill them both in the very room where the Council met. Hastings had already paid the penalty for his share in the plot by being beheaded on Tower Green: the Queen could not be removed from the Sanctuary at Westminster: the Bishop of London would deal with Jane Shore.

The citizens dispersed in great perplexity: and soon after they saw Jane Shore, whose beauty both Edward the Fourth and Lord Hastings were known to have admired only too much, walking barefoot, wrapped in a white sheet, a lighted taper in her hand, even as Duchess Eleanor had walked forty years before.

As the long summer days passed the tension in the City increased. The palace of Westminster re-echoed with the loud cries and clashing of weapons of armed men, and more men, summoned by Gloucester, were hurrying south from York. People must have wondered at the change which had come over Duke Richard, formerly the most loyal and unobtrusive among the royal kinsmen. He had spent less

[1] See Chapter IV, p. 75.

time in London than his brothers Edward the Fourth and
Clarence; at one time he was far away battling with the
Scots, at another he was living peacefully with his young
wife and baby son in Yorkshire. Yet his looks and bearing
were not unfamiliar, his pale, intelligent, rather unhappy
face, his trick of playing nervously with the jewelled ring
on his little finger; and London, having heard no ill of him,
was ready to think well.

On June 22nd, the actual date once named for young
Edward the Fifth's Coronation, a very startling sermon was
preached in the open-air pulpit outside St. Paul's. Few, if
any, of the congregation can have known that on that very
spot the Witenagemot was wont to meet in Anglo-Saxon
times. The preacher put forward two ideas either of which
would, if founded on fact, bar the boy-King from the throne.
First he suggested that Edward the Fourth being already
betrothed to another lady his marriage with Elizabeth
Woodville was unsanctified in the eyes of Holy Church:
and then he hinted that Richard of Gloucester being the only
one of the late Duke of York's sons to be born in England
was also the only one about the circumstances of whose birth
there could be no uncertainty. The congregation listened in
silence, even when Gloucester rode past, as if by chance, and
was hailed from the pulpit as a lifelike image of his father.

Two days later Buckingham came to Guildhall and repeated these arguments to a meeting of citizens, yet when
they were asked if they would have Richard for their King
only a few voices were raised in his favour and those at the
very back of the hall. What we should now call 'propaganda'
was none the less working hard against the poor young Princes
who were half Woodvilles by birth, and a few days later a
deputation arrived at Baynard's Castle begging Richard to
accept the Crown. Parliament soon passed an Act declaring
that the Princes in the Tower were not the lawful heirs of

Edward the Fourth; and it seemed as if a new Plantagenet line were sprouting from a new stem of the White Rose.

For the last three hundred years and more we have watched the march of these events through the eyes of William Shakespeare, whose blood-chilling play of *Richard the Third* was based upon the chronicles of Tudor historians. None of these historians would have dared to write a single word in defence of the last of the Plantagenets, though poor folk in Yorkshire, where he was well known, spoke kindly of him after his death and were harshly punished by the first of the Tudors. Perhaps when the deputation came to ask him to accept the crown he did receive them prayer-book in hand; perhaps he really did say, 'Alas, why would you heap these cares on me?' or words to that effect. Perhaps he contrived, if he did not actually commit the murders of Henry the Sixth, George, Duke of Clarence, Edward, Prince of Wales, Edward the Fifth and the little Duke of York. But no Judge or Jury would convict him on the evidence. Every accused person should be heard before being condemned and Richard has never been allowed to speak. A few things we know. That he was loyal to his brother, King Edward the Fourth, through thick and thin; that during his short reign he ruled wisely and well; and that he was by no means unpopular with the Londoners until their minds were influenced against him. They gave him £1,000 as a coronation gift, and he in return gave to the City a gold cup studded with gems. London highly approved three of the measures taken by his first Parliament; the employment of foreign apprentices was forbidden, the privileges of foreign merchants were curtailed; and the system of 'benevolences' or forced loans was abolished—at any rate for the time being.

It was at this time that the Chief Magistrate of the City began to bear the title of Lord Mayor, which his successors have borne ever since.

Before long, Richard's luck changed. He lost his wife, and then his only son; and certain men whom he trusted, the Duke of Buckingham and Lord Stanley among them, proved traitors. It is curious that he should have put his trust in Lord Stanley, the stepfather of Henry Tudor, Earl of Richmond, a descendant (on the mother's side) of John of Gaunt and a possible claimant to the throne if Richard himself and Clarence's son and daughters were removed. Being of Welsh blood (on his father's side) this quiet, prudent young man had many sympathizers in Wales and in the West but when the faithless Buckingham planned a rising on the Welsh marches the weather fought on Richard's side and the whole thing fizzled out. Buckingham paid with his head for his share in the adventure, but Richard continued to trust Stanley even after Henry Tudor landed at Milford Haven and invaded the Midlands. It was to Stanley's command that he confided the 5,000 men upon whom he counted to win the day for him when the two armies should meet. They met at Bosworth, and at the critical moment the 5,000, led by Lord Stanley, flung themselves into the battle on the side of Henry Tudor.

Richard the Third seems to have enjoyed wearing the crown which he had struggled so hard to win and was fated to wear for so short a time. Many Londoners remembered him appearing in his full regal array at the Christmas festivities in Westminster only eight months before he rode forth to his last fight with the golden circlet upon his helm. After he lay dead, pierced by many wounds, his one-time friend Stanley found the crown hanging in a thornbush, retrieved it, and set it upon the brow of Henry Tudor.

Perhaps because his claim was a doubtful one, perhaps because his descent was not all-royal or even all-noble, Henry the Seventh did not make his entry into London wearing that one unmistakable outward sign of Kingship.

His was no heroic or picturesque figure, but he soon set to work to create a new social order and to bring to his aid a new governing class. Numerous beheadings of peers and abolitions of peerages broke the traditional power of the old nobility. The realm was now to be ruled through the Privy Council in London and the unpaid Justices of the Peace in

Trial of weights and measures under Henry the Seventh

'*He was a good man of affairs, cautious, cold-blooded, clear-eyed*'

From a Manuscript in the British Museum

the country. Though he taxed the people heavily, he was a good man of affairs, cautious, cold-blooded, clear-eyed. The Londoners accepted but they never loved him. Any sentimental corner in the City's heart was occupied by his wife, Elizabeth of York, sister of the two small Princes concerning whose fate so little curiosity seems to have been shown, though it is possible that many prudent people felt doubts which, being prudent, they did not utter.

CHAPTER VI

'Flower of Cities All'

A KING may sometimes have looked with mixed feelings at the great City Companies, which were immensely wealthy and had at their command the Armed Bands, paid and equipped by the City; but they also performed invaluable services, enforcing regulations as to sound craftsmanship and proper weights and measures and developing those commercial interests upon which the whole country was coming more and more to depend. They were the bankers and brokers as well as the merchants and manufacturers of the time, and they were willing to advance money to royal and noble personages in need of it—as such personages were wont to be.

Until Henry the Eighth's quarrel with the Pope changed the form and colour of the City's religion each Guild or Company had its patron Saint. Members were expected to go in procession to church on certain appointed days, and they turned out in full force at the Requiem Mass when one of their number died. A special pall, richly embroidered, was used on such occasions. Priests were paid to pray for the souls of the departed. And when there was a 'riding' the living brethren took part in it, wearing splendid chains and gowns of uniform colours.

These gowns, known as Livery Gowns, were usually of two colours which might be varied from time to time if the Master and the Wardens so pleased. For example, in 1414 the Grocers wore scarlet and green: in 1418, scarlet and black; in 1450, crimson and purple. The Master of each Company also had a pendant jewel to wear during his term of office, and with this he was solemnly invested at his election. But it is wrong to write of these things in the past tense. The Companies, the Liveries, the pendant jewels, and many of the ancient ceremonies are still part of the life of the great City.

The Merchant-Taylors' Pall

Used at the funerals of the members of the Company. Rich brocade and fine embroidery, with a pair of tailors' scissors at each corner

Still in the possession of the Company

When in earlier times a man became a member of a Livery Company he had to promise to be loyal to his craft, obedient to its rules, and 'brotherly' to the other members: but it is sad to think how often brawls broke out between them. The Taylors were particularly aggressive. For example, in the year 1226 they had a street fight with the Goldsmiths, and much blood was shed. In 1415, the year of Agincourt, it was charged against them that they had often 'assembled in great numbers . . . and wounded, beaten and maltreated many lieges of their lord the King.'

The Brewers were especially proud of the fine fat swans

served at their feasts—swan being then as popular as turkey is now—and in 1425 no fewer than twenty-five of these birds graced their table. Round about that time the famous Richard Whittington was harassing this Company, which he accused of overcharging the public for their beer; but the Brewers retorted crossly that it was the excessive splendour of their swan-feasts and not the excessive price of their beer which annoyed Master Whittington.

Arms of the Merchant-Taylors

A tent between two mantles: above, the sacred lamb

From a stained glass window in the Merchant Taylors' Hall

When a Company gave a banquet its badge was to be seen on all sides, wrought in gold or silver, enamel or embroidery, oak or glass. The Grocers' badge was a camel, the Fishmongers', a dolphin, the Poulterers', a pelican, the Merchant Taylors', a tent flanked by two long mantles to show their twofold activities as makers of tents and pavilions in addition to clothes.

More than one Plantagenet King had shown favour to the Taylors, but it was the first Tudor, Henry the Seventh, who raised them to the rank of Merchant Taylors 'in consideration of their having immemorially exercised merchandise in all parts of the globe'.

No man could be a freeman of London or fill any great office there who had not been apprenticed for seven years to some craft. In return for lodging and instruction in his master's house each lad had to promise to serve him faithfully and well, to keep his trade secrets, protect his interests, and abstain from brawling, tippling, and low company.

The Fifteenth-century Crypt of Guildhall

The scene of many stirring scenes in the history of the City

Among·the most important results of Henry the Seventh's state-craft was the marriage of his elder son, Arthur, Prince of Wales, a delicate, good-looking youth, to the pious Spanish Princess Katherine of Aragon, daughter of the powerful sovereigns, Ferdinand and Isabella, whose far-stretched dominions included a large part of the New World discovered by Christopher Columbus. The London merchants fully appreciated what a clever move their pale, unwarlike King had made; and many of them attended the

stately wedding in St. Paul's in 1501. Spain was the keystone
of his carefully planned foreign policy, but he had two
daughters, one of whom he married to King James the Fourth
of Scotland.

Among the Scots who came to negotiate this match was
the poet, William Dunbar. So impressed was he with what
he saw in London that he wrote an admiring poem in which
each of the seven stanzas ends with the line,

London, thou art the flower of cities all!

He describes the 'beryl streams' of the Thames,

Where many a swan doth swim with wingës fair,
Where many a barge doth sail and row with oar,
Where many a ship doth rest with top-royall;[1]

He tells her—

Upon thy lusty Bridge of pillars white
   Be merchantës full royall to behold,
Upon thy streetës goeth many a seemly knight
In velvet gownës and in chains of gold.

Strong be thy walles that about thee standës;
   Wise be the people that within thee dwells;
Fresh is thy river with its lusty strandës,
Blithe be thy churches, well-sounding be thy bells.

Thy famous Mayor, of princely governance,
   With sword of justice thee ruleth prudently.
No Lord of Paris, Venice or Florence
In dignity or honour goes him nigh.

He is example, load-stone and guide,
   Principal patron and rose original,
Above all Mayors as master most worthy.
London, thou art the flower of cities all!

[1] The sail above that known then as the 'top-gallant'.

The Scottish poet evidently did not find the King as impressive as the Lord Mayor; but Henry could spend money lavishly when it suited his plans, and he was well aware of the importance of conciliating the City. At Christmas-time in the year 1494 he entertained the Lord Mayor, Aldermen and principal citizens of London to a great feast in Westminster Hall, followed by 'disguisings and other disports'. Sixty different dishes were served to the King and Queen and forty to the City guests, who returned to London in their state barges and did not arrive there until 'the break of the next day'.

Four years later his second son, the future Henry the Eighth, paid a formal visit to the City. He was then only seven years old, but he made quite a neat little speech of thanks when he was presented with a pair of silver-gilt goblets. Little did the Lord Mayor and Aldermen dream that when this sturdy, red-haired child grew to man's estate he would, by his wilfulness and determination, change the whole face of social and religious life in the realm. Incidentally he changed the face of London, the lives of her citizens, the aims and customs of the great Companies, and the whole course of history. But in 1498 he was a younger son, unlikely ever to wear the crown.

All these royal attentions pleased the Londoners; and they were even better pleased when the new King came to the throne and, as Henry the Eighth, proceeded to hang the two hated tax-collectors, Empson and Dudley, who had been his father's instruments in squeezing money out of the City. Another thing which gave satisfaction to them was his marriage to his brother's widow, Katherine of Aragon, whom everyone liked and respected, and through whom England might expect to enjoy all the advantages of Spanish support against France, to say nothing of trade with the New World.

One of the finest sights of the year in London was the annual procession of the Armed Bands belonging to the City —archers, pikemen, lancers, carabineers, led by the Lord Mayor on horseback and attended by drummers, trumpeters and morris-dancers. In 1510 the King disguised himself as one of his own Yeomen of the Guard and went to see the cavalcade wending its way through streets hung with green garlands. He was so pleased that he made a point of going again, but next time not in disguise, as he took the Queen and almost the whole court with him. A cheerful, popular King, often called 'Hal' or 'Harry' by his loving subjects; had not London good cause to like him well?

When two years later he fell in with the deep-laid plans of his father-in-law, King Ferdinand, and declared war on France, he demanded that London should provide three hundred men-at-arms. Towards their equipment the City Companies subscribed £405. There was as yet no such thing as a regular military uniform, but all these soldiers wore white tunics embroidered with the City arms—the silver shield with St. George's Cross and St. Paul's sword. And just as London merchants had helped to equip the ships of Edward the Third and the archers of Henry the Fifth, they now supplied not only the weapons and the wearing-apparel of the men who fought at the Battle of Spurs but also the rich stuffs which made the Field of the Cloth of Gold famous in legend as well as in history.

Popular though the big, burly King might be, the impression that he protected and favoured the numerous foreign merchants and artificers in London could not fail to dim his popularity a little. These foreigners not only took away trade and employment which rightly belonged to the Londoners; they were arrogant and ill-mannered, and the anger of the people simmered until it boiled over. For example, there was a carpenter named Williamson who bought two pigeons in Cheapside and just as he was about to pay for them a Frenchman came up and said that they were not suitable food for a carpenter. 'Well,' said Williamson, 'I have bought them, and now paid for them, and therefore I will have them.' 'Nay,' said the Frenchman, 'I will have them for my lord the Ambassador': and so, says the old chronicler, 'for better or worse the Frenchman called the Englishman a knave', and carried the pigeons away.

Matters came to a head at Easter, 1516, when Dr. Beale, preaching before the Lord Mayor and Aldermen, said plainly that Englishmen ought to keep their country for themselves, 'as birds defend their nests'. One hopes that the preacher did not foresee the full effects of his sermon, for its result was the scene of riot and destruction known as Evil May Day. The 'prentices raised their dreaded war-cry of 'Clubs, Clubs!' and they, together with others who should have known better, joined the excited mob in pulling down and looting the houses of foreign inhabitants.

The middle and later years of Henry the Eighth's reign were difficult and even dangerous years for London. The citizens had no sympathy with his efforts to divorce Queen Katherine and marry Anne Boleyn. With angry eyes they watched the two crimson-clad Cardinals, Wolsey, haughty and sullen-looking, and Campeggio, the Pope's gout-crippled representative, arriving at Blackfriars Monastery to take part in the 'trial' of the Queen. Nor had they any pity for Wolsey when his failure to negotiate the divorce brought him crashing to the earth under the thunderbolt of the King's wrath. The fact that Anne Boleyn was the granddaughter of a former Lord Mayor may perhaps have appealed to such of them as approved of the King's anti-papal policy. The Lord Mayor of the day and the Aldermen duly attended a water-pageant in honour of her marriage, when fifty barges hung with cloth of gold and cheered by 'trumpets and other melodious instruments' took part in the show; but there was one Londoner who refused firmly to join in any of these festivities—Thomas More, one-time member of Parliament for the City, later Speaker of the House of Commons, and finally Lord Chancellor, Martyr and Saint.

Himself London-born, he had served the citizens well, even in such matters as water-supply and sanitation, then little regarded and even less understood. They loved him, his wit, his wisdom, his courage. They did not love him less because he cracked jokes on every occasion, or because his raiment was not as spruce and splendid as that of his fellow officials. Many sorrowful glances must have been turned towards the Tower when it was known that More was imprisoned there on the perilous charge of refusing to acknowledge the King as the Supreme Head of the Church. A year later the Lord Chancellor's head was hoisted on a pole over London Bridge, and London knew than henceforth nothing would stand between Henry and his vehement desires.

Margaret Roper, More's beloved daughter, contrived somehow to gain possession of the head, which now rests near her own dust in the vault of St. Dunstan's church, Canterbury. The story runs that as she was being rowed through the southern arch of London Bridge she looked at the gruesome object and exclaimed, 'Would God it would fall in my lap as I pass under!' And, as if by a miracle, it fell.

Though it was mainly through the King's quarrel with the Pope that the Reformation took hold upon England, there were many Londoners who were quite ready to accept the new order. Their ancestors had been Lollards, their descendants would be Puritans. When the King destroyed the shrines of St. Mellitus and St. Erkenwald in St. Paul's Cathedral no bold man uttered a word of protest. Many glorious churches were laid in ruins, and their sculptured saints and noble monuments sold for sixpence the cartload. The City Companies acquired the great halls of some of the suppressed religious foundations for their own use, and continued to use them until the great Fire of 1666 swept almost all of them away. Pursuing his feud against Thomas Becket, whose golden shrine at Canterbury had been stripped bare at his behest, the King ordered that the dedication of the

Henry the Eighth distributing Bibles in English

These were printed partly in London and partly in Paris. Copies were placed in every parish church for all the world to read

The frontispiece of the 'Great Bible' of 1539

chapel on London Bridge should be changed, and the paintings and embroideries representing the martyr should either be destroyed or altered beyond recognition. Not long afterwards the beautiful little building was converted into a dwelling-house and tenanted by a grocer who kept cheeses and other eatables in the vaulted undercroft.

As followers of the old and the new religion were hanged and burnt with perfect impartiality, life became more and more difficult and dangerous. Nobody knew what whim would seize the royal mind, or which way it would jump next; but it was very necessary that people who wished to keep their heads upon their shoulders should be ready to jump in the same direction.

Outwardly the City prospered. The merchants and their wives wore clothes of the Court fashion, gorgeous and

The 'Henry Grace d'Dieu'

This ship was King Henry's intimation to foreign naval powers that he intended to protect the merchant fleets of England

From a picture at Greenwich

heavy, with broad, square outlines, quite unlike the narrow slenderness of the earlier style. The 'prentices in their flat woollen caps filled the air with their shrill cries of 'What d'ye lack?' thereby inviting the passers-by to pause. Yet life was different in many ways for many people, both old and young.

All the schools in London had been attached to some religious foundation, and although some of them were re-founded on the new pattern it was long before the cause of education recovered from the blow dealt by a King who professed to be himself a lover of learning. Among those which did survive was St. Paul's,[1] founded in 1509 by Dean Colet. The boys of the Cathedral School, a more ancient school than his, were nicknamed 'Paul's Pigeons'; and they frequently brawled with 'Antony's Pigs', the pupils of a rival establishment in Threadneedle Street, satchels being used as weapons of war. Little seems to have been done for the daughters of the citizens when the nunneries were abolished. In the Priory of St. Helen's, Bishopsgate (and in many other nunneries) these small girls had been taught good manners, fine embroidery, a fragment or two of French and Latin, and how to sing in Church. Theirs was no bleak existence; their relations and friends were allowed to visit them, and discipline cannot have been very severe in the middle of the fifteenth century when they had a Prioress who kept pet dogs and wore a gold hem upon her veil.

It was not until the succession of Henry the Eighth's little red-haired son, Edward the Sixth, that London felt the full rigour of Reform. His mother had been a Seymour; his uncles, her brothers, had enriched themselves with the plunder of ruined Abbeys, and there was nothing they dreaded more than the restoration of the ancient faith. A new English Book of Common Prayer was drawn up, to replace the Latin Missal. There were to be no more candles, images, painted windows, or censers in the bleak churches. Yet even among Protestant-minded Londoners there was reluctance and bewilderment. The Seymours were as un-popular as the Beauforts and the Woodvilles had been, and it seemed that they would rule the City and the country until the young King came to man's estate.

That was fated never to be; and when Edward died at the early age of sixteen London became the centre of the dis-turbing events which followed. King Henry the Eighth's

---

[1] Moved to Hammersmith in 1884.

Will had placed his elder daughter, Mary, next in the line of succession; after her, his younger daughter, Elizabeth; and after *her* the descendants of his sister Mary, Duchess of Suffolk.

Coronation procession of Edward the Sixth passing along Cheapside. The Eleanor Cross can be seen in the centre

After his accession London felt 'the fill rigour of Reform'

Engraving from 'Vetusta Monumenta'

The Protestant nobles on the Council determined to set both Mary and Elizabeth aside and place on the throne the undeniably Protestant Jane Grey, sixteen-year-old grand-daughter of the Duchess of Suffolk. The two Princesses were warned that the Council intended to clap them into the Tower; Mary fled to Framlingham Castle in Suffolk, where she unfurled the royal standard; and Elizabeth, who was at Hatfield, prudently retired to bed.

Mary was half-Spanish. She belonged to the old religion. But she was known to possess the virtues London loved; honesty, courage, generosity. After Lady Jane's troubled reign of nine days the rightful heiress was willingly accepted as Queen.

When Mary, a small, upright, red-haired woman with a rather stern, sorrowful face, approached Aldgate, dressed in violet velvet and riding a white horse, the Lord Mayor and the City companies came in great state to meet her. When, urged on by her kinsman, the Emperor Charles the Fifth, she put Lady Jane on trial for her life, the Londoners may have been sorry for the poor girl, but no rising on her behalf occurred in the City itself, and by leading a revolt of Kentishmen to set her free Sir Thomas Wyatt merely sealed her doom.

Wyatt's rebellion had two aims. To prevent sentence of death from being executed on Jane Grey, and to put an end to the negotiations for a marriage between Mary Tudor and the Emperor's son, Philip the Second of Spain. Times had changed indeed since the citizens had thought a Spanish match the best possible thing.

Wyatt reached Southwark. The Council panicked. Should the Queen flee the country or take refuge in the Tower? Mary would do neither. She rode through London to Guildhall and there, in her gruff Tudor voice, addressed the assembled Londoners. She told them that she was their Queen 'by right, inheritance and law' and that she loved her subjects 'earnestly'. She would never, she said, consent to the Spanish betrothal 'to the danger or loss of any of them'. Let them pluck up their hearts and stand fast by their lawful Prince. They obeyed. The Armed Bands defended London Bridge so manfully that Wyatt's men could not force their way in. Wyatt himself hesitated, and was lost. Lady Jane was lost too. If all the Emperor's councils had been heeded, Elizabeth would have followed them both to the headsman's block on Tower Green.

The fact that London had supported Mary against Wyatt did not mean that the City had been won over to the Spanish match. Already the people were turning towards the young

Shilling of Mary the First

'*Cooing and billing
Like Philip and Mary on a shilling*'

Elizabeth, who continued to play her careful, waiting game with the knowledge that only her sister's mercy stood between her and a criminal's death—and only her sister's life between her and the throne, if no child were born to Philip and Mary.

King Philip, when he came, made great efforts to conquer his natural stiffness and coldness in order to win over the English people. But they objected strongly to seeing him called 'King of England' on the new coinage, and they asked themselves, as time passed, why English blood and English gold should be poured forth to support Spain against

France. And the mood of London hardened when four hundred Londoners of the poorer class were hanged for their alleged share in Wyatt's foolish adventure.

There were worse things in store.

Mary Tudor believed that she was God's chosen instrument to bring England back to the Roman fold. She believed that if she did His will He would send her a son who should be the greatest Christian Prince in history. So within a year of her marriage began the Marian persecution in which, against the advice of the Pope himself, two hundred and eighty-eight victims, rich and poor, women as well as men, were burned alive for refusing to accept the supreme authority of the Church of Rome.

The Lord Mayor and Aldermen were not among them: but when, in robes and chains, they went forth to take part in the ceremonies of the Old Faith they were hooted as they passed through the streets. The Sheriffs were compelled to be present at many of the burnings at Smithfield, but the crowd, nothing daunted, openly voiced their sympathy with the martyrs and their admiration for their constancy. This was a belief for which men were willing to die. Perhaps it was worth dying for?

More than once the Londoners heard without any joy the rumour that a royal child, half-Spanish, half-English, was to be born at Hampton Court. The parish priest of St. Botolph's, Aldgate, preached a sermon in honour of an event which had not happened—and would never happen. And presently it became known that the Queen lay dying in St. James's Palace, the hunting-lodge built by her father when the surrounding marshes teemed with wildfowl. There, as the dim winter dawn broke over Thames one November day in the year 1558, she died, the most unhappy of all the Queens of England.

Why, having been so much disappointed in one woman

sovereign, were the Londoners so willing to welcome the young Elizabeth? The answer is simple enough. Mary represented Rome and Spain as well as England; Elizabeth represented England only. Her sympathy with the Reformers was well known; she was credited with a healthy hatred of Spain; and her subjects were to find that this red-haired, keen-eyed sovereign had inherited the virtues of both the greatest Tudors. She was cautious, astute and economical like her grandfather; she was gorgeous—and, on occasion, bluff—like her father. Londoners loved her from the first day of her reign to the last, and never grew weary of showing her that they did. Shipping on the Thames fired ear-shattering salutes for her; flags flew from steeples, fountains gushed with wine, merchants went in many-coloured processions, to do her honour. Nor should it be forgotten that one of the greatest of the great poets who sang her praises in immortal verse was a Londoner-born. Edmund Spenser, author of the *Faerie Queen* in which Elizabeth figures as the golden-haired, all-conquering Gloriana, was the son of a cloth-maker of East Smithfield. But all these things were still to come when the new Queen was choosing her coronation robe and consulting her astrologer, Dr. John Dee, as to her luckiest day.

The City put forth mighty efforts to greet the new sovereign worthily, and as she passed slowly through the gaily decorated streets on the eve of her coronation she scattered cordial words and gracious smiles on all sides. Children recited pompous poems; musicians made what one chronicler called 'a great noyse'; and in Gracechurch Street there was a group of painted, gilded and draped figures showing Henry the Seventh enclosed in a large red rose, Elizabeth of York his wife enclosed in an equally large white one, and Henry the Eighth, rising from their joined hands upon the stem of a rose both white and red. Henry the

Eighth, wearing his 'crown imperial', was holding the hand of Anne Boleyn, also crowned; and this curious family tree, much bedecked with roses both red and white, continuing upward, bore the likeness of their only child, Elizabeth. That there might be no mistake, the name of each parent was clearly written over the appropriate image. What can the new Queen have felt, as she looked up and saw the name and image of her mother, the same mother whose dishonoured dust was mingled with the dust of other victims of King Hal's cruelty in the vault beneath the small grey chapel on Tower Green? Whatever she felt, she made no sign.

Her canopied litter drawn by two plumy-tailed horses (one in front and one behind) was constantly brought to a halt by pageants and presentations, and she was never at a loss for an apt word. In Cheapside she saw a figure of Father Time with his scythe. 'Time?' she said, quickly, 'And Time hath brought me hither.' When the City Recorder gave to her, on behalf of the City, a crimson satin purse containing a thousand gold marks, she took it in both her long slender hands and bade them all be sure that she would be as good to them 'as ever Queen was to her people'. Seeing an old man in the crowd weeping she exclaimed ''Tis for joy, I warrant you.' When her litter reached Westminster she was perceived to be still holding a sprig of myrtle which an aged dame had thrown to her near the beginning of her progress. The gift of a richly-bound Bible in the English language she received with the assurance that she 'would oftentimes read over that Book'.

As time passed the Lord Mayor and Aldermen developed an appetite for sermons as long and as heavy as their longest and heaviest banquets. The Queen liked sermons too, but to please her they had to be learned, uncontroversial—and not too long. She also liked stage-plays, which the City Fathers frowned upon. No one frowned upon the savage and popular 'sport' of tying a bull or a bear to a stake and unleashing fierce dogs to attack it. Elizabeth found it most entertaining.

If the ghost of a citizen of Londinium Augusta had re-visited the south bank of the Thames he would have found bull-rings and bear-gardens in full swing where wild beast fights had been held more than a thousand years before. He would have found none of the careful town-planning of his own time, no well paved streets, no drainage system, no central heating; but he would have seen gay and gorgeous colour everywhere. Though coal was now being brought by sea from Newcastle, whence the Elizabethan term 'sea-coal', it had not yet begrimed the face of London—a face decorated with carving and gilding, plaster work, paint and elaborate designs in timber, and much more picturesque though less dignified than the austere colonnades of the Roman City.

Round St. Paul's had gathered the shops and stalls of the booksellers whose trade, in spite of watchful government censorship, flourished then as never before. In the nave ebbed and flowed a murmuring, many-coloured tide of people certainly not drawn thither by any religious thoughts. Some went to hire servants or sell horses, some to plot mis-chief or cadge a free meal; some went to gossip with their friends, show off a new starched ruff or a new embroidered doublet. Shakespeare makes Sir John Falstaff say of Bardolph his red-nosed hanger-on, 'I got him in Paul's'; and Shake-speare's contemporary, Thomas Dekker, describes how a young dandy who wished the fame of his fashionable attire to be spread through the City by the cathedral choristers would go up into the chancel holding his embroidered purse ready to 'quoit' silver into their hands, while they swarmed about him 'like so many white butterflies'.

CHAPTER VII

Elizabeth the First and her Londoners

THE London of Elizabeth the First was still a medieval City. Its narrow, irregular streets and small, low-pitched dwellings were ill-fitted to contain a population growing every year in numbers and in prosperity. In 1580 Her Majesty was induced by the considered opinion of 'the Lord Mayor, Aldermen and other grave, wise men' to issue a Proclamation suggesting a remedy. Perceiving that multitudes of people were 'heaped up together and in a sort smothered', she forbade the building of any new house or tenement within three miles of the gates, and also decreed that only one family should inhabit each house. What was to happen to the sub-tenants thus sternly ejected is not made clear.

Along the Strand, along Cheapside, and all about St. Paul's the shop signs swung and creaked. Jonah and the whale, a child in the claws of an eagle, a lily in bloom, a mermaid, a swan, a rising sun, were only a few of these gaily painted and gilded devices. Merchandise from all over the known world could be bought beneath their shadow: and not only merchandise. At the Sign of the Silver Pelican a French Protestant refugee kept a day-school where for five shillings a week boys were instructed in the Latin and French languages, an extra three shillings a month being charged if the pupil took his midday meal at school.

Sir Thomas Gresham, one of the first City worthies to be received by the Queen, had served her sister Queen Mary overseas, and had spent some time in the great trading centre of Antwerp, in the Spanish Netherlands. There he had been much impressed by the institution known as the Bourse, where merchants might meet to do business and merchandise could be stored and shown. There was also a Bourse in Venice, but as yet there was nothing similar in London. Gresham decided that it was high time to set this right. In June, 1566, he had the happiness of laying the first brick of the great Exchange in Cornhill which, with the active support of the City Companies, he had planned and brought into being.

The Gresham family crest, a grasshopper, appeared in bronze or stone at many points—on the top of the bell-tower, above the upper windows, and surmounting a lofty pillar which overlooked the quadrangle. Round this quadrangle ran covered walks where merchants met in wet weather, and where more than a hundred small shops set forth their wares to tempt the passer-by. Apothecaries, selling mysterious drugs from distant lands, goldsmiths, book-sellers, armourers, all traded busily there; but such small things as mouse-traps, birdcages, lanterns and shoe-horns could also be found by those who needed them.

January 23rd, 1570, was a great day for the City, when the Queen herself dined with Sir Thomas Gresham at his hand-some house in Bishopsgate and afterwards visited the Bourse, which she 'viewed on every side'. To the sound of a trumpet blown by a herald in his richly-coloured tabard, it was pro-claimed for all to hear that the place was henceforth to be known as the 'Royal Exchange'. The original building perished in the Great Fire of 1666; its successor was burned to the ground in 1838; but a third, opened in 1844, still bears the name bestowed by Elizabeth the First more than three hundred years ago.

Unluckily Sir Thomas Gresham's idea of a grave and

dignified meeting-place for grave and dignified men did not turn out exactly as he planned. On Sundays and holidays rough boys and noisy children used to run about among the pillared walks, shouting so loudly that the congregation of the nearest church could not hear the sermon. A tavern-keeper was fined for 'broiling herrings, sprats and bacon to the vexation of the worshipful merchants resorting to the Exchange'. They were also much disturbed by the loud cries of women selling apples and oranges at the Cornhill entrance. None the less 'worshipful merchants' continued to transact business there, and their wives soon found it an excellent place to spend an idle hour or two, gossip with their friends, and make purchases large or small.

The maid of such a wife might well spend two or three hours of every day preparing her mistress to walk abroad. The cheeks were painted, the head was trimmed and tricked with 'bolsters' of false hair upon which were fixed garlands of gold and silver tinsel; the ruff, a huge, three-tiered erection, had to be as stiff as if it were carved out of fretted ivory. In her hand the dame might carry a fan, a shopping-satchel or a pomander,[1] according to the hour of the day and her plans for that hour. If she went forth after dusk it was the duty of one of her husband's apprentices to escort her, carrying a lantern.

In a Puritan household, things were ordered otherwise. The dress of the housewife was severely simple, her habits were thrifty and industrious; and she kept a stern eye on the young 'prentices, who, as well she knew, preferred a stage-play or a bear-baiting to a six-hour-long sermon at Paul's Cross.

In one of the comedies of the period, *The Shoemakers' Holiday* by Thomas Dekker, we get a vivid picture of the daily round in a London shop. The principal character,

[1] An apple-shaped container, sometimes of silver or even gold, filled with sweet spices

Simon Eyre, was a real Lord Mayor, who lived in the fifteenth century and was long remembered because he
gave a pancake feast to all the 'prentices in the City on the
day of his election: but the shoemakers in Dekker's story are
pure Elizabethans. We hear Eyre, a noisy, merry fellow,
calling to his lads to wake up and open the shop-windows
and sweep the street outside. Groaning with reluctance
Fisk and Hodge rise from their pallets under the counter.
'O Master, good morrow,' said Hodge, 'You are an early
stirrer. I could have slept this hour. Here's a fine day
coming.' 'Master,' says Fisk, 'let *us* pray for good leather,
and let ploughboys and those that work in the fields pray
for fine days. What care *I* if it rains?' Later we see them
helping to dress him in his new gown of embossed damask
and velvet; and finally we behold him welcomed to the office
of Lord Mayor by 'The King' in person (no particular
King), to whom he apologizes for his uncourtly manners.
'Nay,' answers the King,

> *I pray thee, good Lord Mayor, be even as merry*
> *As if thou wert among thy shoemakers.*
> *It does me good to see thee in this humour.*

In their own trade journeymen-hatters were described as
'gentlemen' long before that term was so freely scattered
about as it is today. Tradition says that on one occasion
Queen Elizabeth was welcomed in Holborn by 'a great
congregation of well-dressed men wearing polished beaver
hats'. The Queen, struck by their neat and flourishing
appearance, asked who they might be. She was told that
these were the journeymen-hatters of Southwark and Blackfriars. 'Such journeymen', she answered, 'must be gentlemen.'

One day in the year 1572 the Bishop of London drew up
a list of nine things to be done for the protection of the realm.

The first was 'forthwith to cutte off the Scottish Queen's heade'—that unfortunate Queen who had already pined for two years in captivity and would pine for fifteen more before her English kinswoman acted upon the Bishop's advice. In the interval Elizabeth never ceased to encourage and reward the bold seafarers who challenged the Spanish monopoly of

Elizabeth the First

'*Gorgeous, arrogant, enigmatic Queen*', *much loved by her Londoners to her life's end*

After a portrait by Isaac Oliver

trade in the New World. London was deeply interested in these ventures, and the fact that Philip of Spain was the champion of Mary, Queen of Scots, added to the general satisfaction when the battered ships cast anchor off Deptford heavy with the spoils of their audacity.

The story of the struggle against Spain is part of the story of England, but London bore her part in it—and so did London's Queen. Like the great City Companies, Elizabeth invested money in these expeditions, and like them she collected her profits in due course, though keeping carefully in the background all the while. Once, however, she did come boldly forward as the patroness of the greatest pirate of the whole far-journeying brotherhood. This was in April, 1579 when the Londoners beheld with their own eyes the *Golden Hind* in which Francis Drake had sailed all round the globe—the first Englishman to perform that feat.

The Queen believed firmly in Drake's lucky star; but when the Spanish Ambassador protested in the name of King Philip against the 'lawless, bloody and piratical' deeds of her seamen, she faltered for a moment. Then news came which dispelled any misgivings she may have felt. After an absence of two years the *Golden Hind* cast anchor off Deptford. The little ship, sole survivor of the five which had sailed out of Plymouth in 1577, was low in the water with her heavy cargo of treasure, the spoils of a journey quite correctly described in the words of the Spanish Ambassador quoted above.

The delighted Queen gave orders that this fairy-tale cargo of gold and gems should be shifted to the Tower. She allotted ten thousand pounds to the Captain as his share; and she decided to visit the *Golden Hind*, to dine on board, and to knight Francis Drake on the deck, in full view of the crowds of excited Londoners thronging the river bank. It was a resounding slap upon King Philip's face, and the onlookers greeted it with shouts of approval.

It was not only in the Spanish possessions of the New World that the Londoners were interested. In May, 1557, when Philip and Mary still reigned, four English ships left Gravesend to convoy back to the far-off land of 'Muscovy' a trade delegation from its Emperor, Ivan the Terrible. Out of that Russian visit to London grew the Russia Company, which was actively encouraged by the far-seeing Elizabeth.

The Captain of the four ships, Anthony Jenkinson, landed his passengers safely at Archangel, and then proceeded to Moscow, where he was equally impressed by the squalor and the splendour of Ivan's court. He returned to Russia in 1561, and was the first Englishman to sail the Caspian Sea. Armed with personal letters from the Queen, he succeeded (though not without considerable difficulty) in obtaining safe conducts and trading privileges from both the Emperor of Russia and the Shah (whom he calls the 'Sophy') of Persia.

The Sophy, wrote Jenkinson,

demanded of me of what country of Franks[1] I was, and what affaires I had there to do? Unto whom I answered that I was of the famous Citie of London within the noble Realme of England, and that I was sent thither from the most excellent and gracious soveraigne Lady Elizabeth . . . for to treat of friendship and free passage of our merchants and people to repair and traffique within his dominions.

Largely owing to disturbed conditions in the Near East the Russia Company did not prosper quite as much as its members had hoped that it might. The Dutch later challenged its monopoly of the Spitzbergen Whale-Fisheries, and later still the execution of Charles the First so shocked the Russian Emperor of the time that he refused to have any more dealings with England till after the restoration of Charles the Second. It was otherwise with the East India Company, to which Queen Elizabeth granted a charter in 1600, and which lasted till 1858, when under an Act for the better Government of India, it relinquished its power to the Crown.

The City Companies were now filling the gaps made by Henry the Eighth's destruction of the ancient monastic schools. Christ's Hospital, Newgate (better known as the

---

[1] The term used in the East for the Christian nations in general.

Blue Coat School[1]), seems to have been an object of interest to individual citizens as well as to civic bodies. Sir William Chester, a Lord Mayor, at his own expense arched over an evil-smelling ditch which poisoned the air breathed by the boys, and a shoemaker called Castell, noted for his early rising, bequeathed to Christ's Hospital £44 from his hard-earned store.

It was not only the Merchants and the City Companies who founded schools; a famous one was built and endowed by a certain Dame Alice Owen, whose father was a Londoner and two of whose three husbands were London merchants.

One fine day, when young Alice was walking with her maid near the butts at Islington where the citizens practised archery, she came upon a woman milking a cow and insisted on taking over the stool and milking-pail. It was a girlish whim, but it had results to be seen today. When Alice rose from the stool a stray arrow passed right through her high-crowned hat. 'If', she exclaimed, 'I live to be a lady I will some day erect some building on this very ground in consideration of the great mercy shown to me by the Almighty!'

The vow was fulfilled, but not until she was widowed for the third time, and not before her faithful maid had jogged her memory. She then bought ten acres of land at Islington, founded a school and some almshouses, and bequeathed to the Brewers' Company the funds needed to maintain both. Her gabled and mullioned Tudor buildings were pulled down in 1840, but she still has pensioners in Islington and outside the modern school which bears her name her statue stands, in high-crowned hat, ruff, and stiff Elizabethan gown.

One cold February day in the year 1586 Londoners learnt that their Bishop's advice had been followed, and that 'the Scottish Quene's heade' had been 'cutte off' at last. Little

[1] The school was moved to Horsham in Sussex in 1902, but the boys still wear the long-skirted, leather-belted blue coats, yellow stockings and buckled shoes which were the habitual attire of their Tudor predecessors.

pity was felt for her, and less still when it became known that she had bequeathed to Philip of Spain her claim to the throne of England. Don Philip, a hard-working, earnest man, was soon busily building huge golden galleons and massing troops and guns for the invasion of the kingdom which he regarded as his own.

In March, 1587 the Queen politely requested the Lord Mayor to train and equip a force of 10,000 men in addition to the 4,000 already under arms. They were soon marching and drilling, the traditional white tunics with the City arms on back and breast showing to the world who and what they were. Officers dressed in black rode beside them; drums and trumpets went before. London also provided and manned sixteen ships and four light pinnaces for Drake's famous pounce on Cadiz, when, in his own homely words, 'he singed the King of Spain's beard'.

Londoners were very conscious of the care and the courage of their Queen during the anxious spring and summer of 1588. They crowded to Tilbury when she rode there to review her troops; they listened to her powerful voice, so like her father's, proclaiming that she had 'the heart of a King, and of a King of England, too'.

But already the 'magnificent, huge and mighty fleet of the Spaniards, such as sayled not upon the Ocean-sea many hundreth yeeres before', had 'vanished in smoake'. Those words, written by a man who remembered the defeat of the Armada, sum up briefly and vividly the complete destruction of King Philip's proud golden galleons.

And then Elizabeth was in their midst again, going in procession to St. Paul's to return thanks to God. Dearly did she love splendour (even her night-caps were sewn with spangles) and willingly did she gratify the Londoners' love of pomp and pageantry as, her raiment winking with rich jewels, she moved slowly along the Strand and up Ludgate

Hill in a chariot drawn by four white horses. No more foreign menaces now, no more Continental problems. England was an island at last, and she and her Queen were worthy of each other.

The voyages of her seafarers had kindled a new and lively interest in the history of her kingdom. In spite of the frowns

The Globe Theatre on Bankside

The 'Wooden O' in which many of Shakespeare's greatest plays were first acted. The hoisting of the flag showed that a performance was about to begin

of the Lord Mayor and Aldermen, Puritans almost to a man, Londoners crowded to the circular wooden theatres at Southwark to watch long historical dramas full of shouting and sword-play. The City authorities seem to have been rather pleased than otherwise when an outbreak of the plague justified them in shutting down the too-popular playhouses. The plague, they said, was sent by God to punish people for their sins; the theatres were great causes of sinfulness; therefore the theatres, being responsible for the plague, must not be allowed to lure the foolish to the south bank of the Thames. It was unfortunate that the Queen and some of her most powerful courtiers should have taken certain companies of play-actors under their protection; it made things much more difficult for the Lord Mayor.

The hoisting of a flag announced that the performance was about to begin; the lowering of the flag showed that it was over. The audience arrived early, and while they waited would play cards, eat nuts and apples, and even try to read books bought from one of the stalls in St. Paul's churchyard the same day. Fashionable young men had stools upon the stage itself, disturbed the actors by cracking nuts, choked them with smoke from that new-fangled toy, a clay pipe, and sometimes dismayed them by rising up and departing with a 'screwed and discontented face' in the middle of the play. People standing in the pit also ate apples, and would pelt with the cores any unlucky mummer who failed to please.

The stage jutted out so that the audience surrounded it on three sides. Apart from screens and curtains there was little scenery, but there were various 'properties' such as mossy banks, four-post beds, dragons, trees, even blue linen clouds. The tragic actors often wore the cast-off finery of the 'gallants'. Jigs, ballads, comic interludes and tunes on the pipe and tabor (one performer playing both instruments, like Ariel in *The Tempest*) relieved the strain of listening to sombre tragedies; and part-songs, exquisitely sung, added to the charm of the comedies. It was a musical age. A lute hung in every barber's shop so that any customer who cared to do so might play a tune while waiting to take his place in the barber's chair.

Poets, many of them destined to be immortal, teemed in the London of Elizabeth. They were drawn from all classes;

courtiers of long descent like Sir Philip Sidney, gentlemen-
adventurers like Sir Walter Raleigh, burghers' sons like
Spenser, Shakespeare and Marlowe, humbly-born rhymesters
who provided the doggerel for Kempe and Tarleton, the
two most popular 'comics' of the day. Every playwright
was in some degree a poet. The same London audience
which demanded gibbering ghosts and gory murders,
nimble jigs and rough horseplay, could and did enjoy the
loveliest verse ever written in the English tongue. And they
could find pleasure in country scenes such as the sheep-
shearing feast in *A Winter's Tale*.

As the golden years passed the affection of the people for
their Queen never waned,

> *Their gorgeous, arrogant, enigmatic Queen*
> *Who held the heart of England as Kings hold*
> *Their jewelled orbs.*

They often saw her, not only in state processions but also
when she graced a wedding with her glittering presence or
visited some highly-honoured subject. In 1594 she attended
a Masque at Gray's Inn, whose members, she said, 'did always
study for some sports to present unto her'. In Ely Place she
would visit her kinsman, Sir Christopher Hatton, the Lord
Chancellor, whose skill in dancing she admired: to the
Strand she would come to sit by the curtained bed of her
Lord High Treasurer, Lord Burleigh, when he was laid up
by a sharp attack of gout. Once, when he apologized for
his infirmity, she answered, 'My lord, we make use of you
not for the badness of your legs but for the goodness of your
head.'

Though Edmund Spenser wrote of the Temple as

> *Those bricky towers*
> *The which on Thames' broad aged back do ride,*
> *Where now the studious lawyers have their bowers,*

the younger lawyers were gay as well as studious, fond of masques and revels, and patrons of professional players. In 1603 the Lord Chamberlain's company performed Shakespeare's *Twelfth Night* in Middle Temple Hall.

Three years earlier the same company had performed the same play before the Queen. She was ageing then, her teeth

Elizabeth the First

Gracing a wedding with her glittering presence

From a contemporary painting

were turning black or falling out, her dead-white, falcon-keen face was criss-crossed by tiny wrinkles; but she wore a dress as youthful as the bride's own at the wedding of Lord Herbert to the only daughter of John, Lord Russell, in June 1600, and even joined in the dance which followed the ceremony. Yet she can have been in no dancing mood, for it was in the same month that the last and perhaps the dearest of her favourites, the young Earl of Essex, was put on trial for the blunders he had committed when sent to Ireland to suppress rebellion two years before.

London was closely concerned with the unhappy story. Her citizens had roared applause when Shakespeare, in the prologue to the last act of his *Henry the Fifth*, painted an imaginary picture of the victorious return of the 'General of their gracious Empress'.

> now behold
> How London doth pour forth her citizens,
> The Mayor and all his brethren in best sort
> Like to the Senators of Ancient Rome,
> With the plebeians swarming at their heels,
> Go forth to fetch their conquering Caesar in!

The reality was not like that at all. When Essex did return it was hastily and by stealth, a discredited man. His enemies, of whom he had many, persuaded the Queen that he was a rebel, if not a traitor; he was put on trial, condemned to relinquish all the rich offices he held, and to remain a prisoner during the Queen's pleasure. She soon relented: he was set free, and allowed to take up his quarters at his magnificent house in the Strand, where the name 'Essex Street' still marks the site. But he would not keep quiet, and he had foolish friends who pricked him on. One of these, Lord Southampton, was attacked in the Strand one day early in 1601 by his arch-foe Lord Grey, and might have been murdered had not a shout of 'Clubs!' brought 'prentices and other townsfolk to the rescue.

Presently word came to Burleigh's brilliant hunchback son, Robert Cecil, then Secretary of State, that Essex had planned to appear suddenly, with a handful of friends, at Paul's Cross on a Sunday when the Lord Mayor, Aldermen and City Companies would be attending an open-air sermon. The rash young man hoped to persuade the citizens that evil counsellors were seeking his life and endangering the Queen's: and then he meant to lead them to Westminster, overwhelm his enemies at Court, and fling himself at his sovereign's feet.

Hearing these things, the Queen ordered the Lord Mayor and other worthies to keep away from Paul's Cross that day,

James the First and Sixth

He loved book-learning and hunting with equal ardour

From a contemporary print

and bade them see to it that the people stayed indoors. They obeyed. Essex, galloping wildly up Ludgate Hill, found the cathedral precincts deserted; when he shouted, 'For the Queen, my mistress! Follow me, good people, follow me!' a very few voices cried out, 'God bless your honour', but no one attempted to follow him.

He was put on trial again, this time for his life, and with his life he paid the forfeit for his folly. And his folly had been very great. All London soon knew that among his crimes was that of holding secret communication with the King of Scots, Mary Stuart's son: but few people knew that he had spoken slightingly of the Queen's altered looks. The two things together sealed his doom.

As time passed Londoners saw their Queen less and less often. From the old red palace at Richmond conflicting rumours travelled downstream. Now she was said to be 'set on jollity'; now it seemed she could not sleep, but would sit alone in the dark, weeping for Essex. The City, through its Members of Parliament, had frequently urged her to marry and so secure the Protestant succession against any possible Popish claimant overseas; but she never agreed, though once or twice it seemed as if she might. For whom would the Lord Mayor carry the crystal sceptre at the next Coronation? Probably for a Scotsman of whom little was known except that he loved booklearning and hunting with equal ardour.

In the dark early hours of March 24th, 1603, the great heart of England's Elizabeth ceased to beat. Her loyal Londoners, as heavily draped in black as the four horses which drew her funeral car, watched with sorrowful faces as the procession passed on its way to Westminster, the waxen-faced, golden-clad effigy of the Queen jolting on the top of her coffin, the twelve proud standards borne on either side by hooded mourners.

CHAPTER VIII

Dark Skies over London

THE people of London, having welcomed in the
course of their history kings from Normandy,
Anjou and Wales, now found themselves compelled
to receive a king from the neighbouring northern kingdom
of the Scots.

As James, with his tall, dark-eyed, flaxen-haired Danish
Queen and their promising little son, Prince Henry, travelled
southward by easy stages in the bright summer weather of
1603 the Londoners made suitable preparations against their
arrival. Six triumphal arches were set up, their allegorical
designs so chosen as to please a king who was known to be
a sound classical scholar and believed to be a pillar of the
Reformed Faith.

But the ill luck of the Stuarts intervened. The hot weather
bred an outbreak of the plague; the traditional procession
from the Tower to Westminster had to be abandoned; and
His Majesty had to come by water, in Queen Elizabeth's
state barge.

A City rhymester of this time grieved over the money
spent uselessly by London;

> *Thousands of treasure hath her bounty wasted*
> *In honour of her King, to welcome him:*
> *But woe is she! that honour is not tasted,*
> *For royal James on silver Thames doth swim:*
> *The water hath that glory, for he glides*
> *Upon those pearly streams unto his Crown.*

Owing to the plague only the Lord Mayor and twelve of the Aldermen attended his coronation, and they, too, 'swam', on the silver Thames to Westminster.

London, now a Puritan stronghold, had hoped that a king educated by that fierce and famous Reformer, George Buchanan, would introduce a new form of worship on the lines favoured at Geneva, abolishing 'prelacy', or church government by Bishops, and making the sermon the most important element in divine service. 'No Bishop, no King,' said James; and he soon made it clear that he intended to be to the Church of England what the translators of the Authorized Version of the Bible called him—'a most tender and loving nursing father'. This translation, begun and carried on under his active supervision, was the greatest achievement of his reign. Even the Puritans could find no fault with it. It was his zeal for prelacy that they disliked. And soon they were comparing to a horde of caterpillars and a plague of locusts the hungry and hopeful Scots who came streaming southward into London.

None the less, those citizens who came into direct contact with him found his hearty, though hardly dignified, manners not altogether unpleasing. For example, when he was enrolled in the Clothworkers' Company he clapped his hands gleefully, and exclaimed with his strong Scottish accent, 'Now I am a Clothworker!' Upon this the Merchant Taylors became envious: they brought forth and showed to the King *their* roll of members, a most impressive document. The King promptly decreed that his elder son, Henry, Prince of Wales, should be enrolled as a Merchant Taylor.

This serious-minded, rather Puritanical young Prince was the idol of Londoners. They had opportunities of seeing him not only on occasions of state but also when he visited the house in Fleet Street where business connected with his own Duchy of Cornwall was transacted. The house still stands, still adorned both inside and out with the Prince of Wales's feathers.

It was perhaps natural that, as his own difficulties increased, the King should have betrayed an occasional touch of jealousy: but nothing could have been more false or more cruel than the rumour which hinted that he had caused his too-popular son to be poisoned. Many Londoners believed that it was so. Some of them whispered that Spain—yes, and Rome—had been in the plot. They found something mysterious in the sudden death of that stern young Protestant. Had they not beheld with their own eyes a lunar rainbow, strange and sinister, in the sky over St. James's Palace when he lay dying there?

They could see the hand of Rome clearly enough in that undoubted plot of which small boys still remind the people of London every year on November 5th—the Gunpowder Plot: and they were quite properly shocked at the wickedness of the small band of conspirators who had planned to blow up the King, Lords and Commons 'in Parliament assembled'. But James's narrow escape did not make them any more obliging when he wanted to borrow money. As London grew richer, kings grew poorer, and the balance of power continued to shift from inherited might to accumulated money.

On one occasion it is said that James was so much annoyed at the refusal of the City of London to lend him the sum of £20,000 that he threatened to move Parliament, the Law Courts and the royal court to Winchester or Oxford. The Lord Mayor in reply observed that the merchants of London would in that event have one consolation—His Majesty could not take the River Thames with him.

Lovers of old London cherish the memory of John Stow, tailor, antiquary and historian, who died in the second year of King James's reign. His Survey is a veritable mine of information, but while making it he appears to have neglected his needle, scissors and thread, for he fell into poverty in his latter years. His widow was none the less able to erect to his memory a handsome monument in the Church of St. Andrew Undershaft where every year on the anniversary of his death a new quill pen is ceremonially placed in his carved right hand.

'*Gunpowder Treason*'

The vault beneath the House of Lords where Guy Fawkes planted his barrels of gunpowder

Always odd and sometimes foolish though King James might be, he honestly desired the good of his people. He planted mulberry trees to encourage the cultivation of silk-worms and the manufacture of silk: and he rendered a signal service to the whole population of the capital by his active encouragement of that enterprising London goldsmith, Hugh Myddleton, in his great enterprise of bringing water to the capital from the springs of Chadwell in Hertfordshire, thirty-eight miles away. This entailed the digging of a canal, known as the New River, and the construction of many drains, sewers and bridges. Hollowed-out trees were used instead of metal pipes, and remnants of these are sometimes unearthed to this day. The City Fathers of London had not the wisdom to support this scheme, but the 'British Solomon' was wiser. He agreed to pay half the cost of the works if Myddleton would give him a half-share in the profits.

Great public rejoicings marked the moment when the waters of the New River first flowed into the cistern prepared for them at Clerkenwell. The Lord Mayor (who happened to be Hugh Myddleton's brother) and Aldermen were present. The workmen who had carried out the difficult and laborious task, all 'well apparrelled', and carrying spades, shovels and pickaxes, marched three times round the cistern, to the sound of drums and trumpets, after which their foreman read aloud a piece of very bad poetry, praising Sir Hugh's 'industry, cost and care' and also the 'King's most gracious love'. Then, says the chronicler John Stow, 'the stream ran gallantly into the cisterne, drummes and trumpets sounding in a triumphall manner, and a brave peale of chambers[1] gave full issue to the intended entertainment'.

It was not only in such things as the cultivation of silk and the distribution of water that James meddled actively with the affairs of Londoners. Peace abroad and harmless pleasure at home were his two chief aims. And in 1618 he published his *Book of Sports* in which he declared that after divine service on Sundays his good people were not to be deterred from lawful recreation and exercise. He granted to his groom-porter, Clement Cottell, the right to license no fewer than forty taverns in London and Westminster (and within a radius of two miles therefrom) where people might play at lawful games, such as bowls, tennis, cards, or 'any

[1] Artillery.

other games thereafter to be invented'. In the *Book of Sports* he commends archery, vaulting, morris-dancing and the setting-up of maypoles.

As the Puritans had been angrily attempting to abolish just such recreations, they hummed like a swarm of hornets when the *Book of Sports* was issued. Most of the City clergy

King James going in procession to St. Paul's

The text over the arch shows the loyalty of the City; the shield and flag declare its independence

From a contemporary print

stubbornly refused to obey the royal command to read aloud the hated book from their pulpits. Nor were the citizens in the least pacified by the King's question as to *when* the common people should have 'leave to exercise' if *not* upon Sundays and holy days, 'seeing they must apply their labour and win their living in all working days'.

The Londoners disliked the King's foreign policy as much as they did his other ideas. They did not agree that a match between his only surviving son, Charles, Prince of Wales, and a Spanish Princess would be a master stroke; and though they shared his uneasiness about his only daughter, Elizabeth, whose husband had been driven out of his kingdom of Bohemia by Spain and the other great Powers of the Catholic League, they would have preferred to vote money and send men to her rescue instead of trying by diplomacy to detach the King of Spain from his allies. Their resentment was great when once again, as in Mary Tudor's days, they saw Spanish envoys driving proudly through the streets.

There were incidents. A 'prentice, watching Count Gondomar being carried in his chair down Fleet Street, shouted out 'There goes the Devil in a dungcart!' For this he and seven of his fellows were sentenced to be whipped through the City. Three hundred indignant 'prentices rose up and set them free. But the mood of London changed when the young Prince and his flashy, flamboyant friend, the Duke of Buckingham, returned from a mysterious trip to Spain with the news that the Spanish match was definitely 'off'.

The Prince was disliked for his cold manners, the Duke, for his pride and his parade of more than royal splendour;[1] but now bonfires blazed in their honour, toasts were drunk, cheers were raised—simply because they had failed in what they set out to do.

King James died in March, 1625, and his funeral, which cost more than £50,000, provided the Londoners with a fine if gloomy spectacle. Nine thousand mourners received their black cloaks free of charge. The hearse looked like a black wedding cake, and was stuck as full of flags as a pincushion could be with pins. It was designed by Inigo Jones, the royal architect, whose duties included the planning of scenery and costumes for the Queen's masques, and whose great Banqueting Hall is all that now remains of his archi-

[1] The water-gate of his vanished mansion is still to be seen in the Embankment Gardens.

tectural work for the King. This hall replaced an earlier one, burnt to the ground in 1619. Sad to relate, a mob of Londoners then broke into the palace of Whitehall during the fire and stole everything within their reach—including the King's bed, which must have been carried boldly away while honest folk were battling vainly with the flames.

King Charles's frequent clashes with the City of London formed a sort of overture to the Civil War. When Buckingham's astrologer, Dr. Lambe, was butchered by the London mob, the King imposed a heavy fine on the City for not finding and punishing the murderers. When plate and jewels belonging to his pretty young French wife, Henrietta Maria, were stolen, he sternly enforced a previous but disregarded edict compelling all goldsmiths to return to their former headquarters in Cheapside, on the plea that being dispersed over the City they offered opportunities for the 'passing away of stolen plate'. More unpopular still were the steps taken by the King and Archbishop Laud to regulate the services of the Church. The wearing of a white surplice, the railing-round of the communion table, the kneeling to receive the Sacrament, all these things smacked of Popery. Numerous new sects were springing up, fanatical, intolerant, sometimes very peculiar. And the westward urge felt by the pilgrims who sailed in the *Mayflower* in 1620 would draw many Londoners across the sea to the New World. It is an interesting point that in the year 1635 twenty-seven such pilgrims left the parish of St. Mildred, Bread Street—the parish in which was born the greatest of all Puritans—John Milton.

The wealth of the nation was now concentrated in the City and from this it followed that no king could reign unless he had the City solidly behind him. Unfortunately Charles the First, in his desperate attempts to raise the funds needed to carry on the government of the country, made one blunder after another, each of which was marked and re-sented by the merchants of London. Particularly did they resent the tax known as Ship Money, although a strong Navy was more important to them than to any other section of the community. There was also the question of the Irish 'plantations' which the late King had induced them to finance

Great Seal of Charles the First

In the background, a glimpse of the north bank of the Thames, London Bridge, etc. The figure is not meant to be a portrait, and the hound is more lifelike than its master

British Museum

and which were now taken away from them on the plea that these had been badly administered. And there were those costly and inglorious expeditions to Cadiz and La Rochelle and the Ile de Rhé, for which all the blame was thrown upon their commander, the Duke of Buckingham.

On a certain Sunday morning in the year 1628 news came from Portsmouth which spread like wildfire through London. Even the congregations in the City churches heard it. In the ancient Church of St. Dunstan's-in-the-West the shock caused two women parishioners to faint—they were the mother and sister of the Puritan, John Felton, who had stabbed Buckingham to death on the eve of his embarkation for another expedition against the French.

The spotlight of popular hatred was next directed upon a very different type of man—Thomas Wentworth, Earl of Strafford, who was as firm as Buckingham was foolish, and who brought to affairs of state a temper as resolute as Archbishop Laud showed in dealing with the affairs of religion. As Lord Deputy of Ireland he had been notably stern, though he was able to boast that under his rule 'no hair of any man's head was touched for the free exercise of his conscience'. When it became clear that he was likely to attempt to deal with England as he had with Ireland, Parliament, strongly supported by the City of London, determined to lay him low. He was impeached on a ridiculous charge of treason; and when, on the unsupported evidence of his enemy, Sir Harry Vane, he was accused of having said that the King had an army in Ireland which might be used for the subjection of 'this kingdom', his fate was sealed. Nobody was willing to believe that by 'this kingdom' he really meant Scotland, where trouble had broken out following the King's unwise effort to force the Book of Common Prayer upon the Scots.

Many London merchants signed a petition that 'the Bill for killing' Strafford should go through. Parliament was implacable. The London mob, howling for blood, broke the windows of the Palace at Whitehall: and it seems quite possible that if Charles had intervened to save his faithful servant, Parliament's next step would have been to impeach his much-loved but foolish little Queen. After a struggle he yielded: and on the night of Strafford's execution the streets of London were full of excited citizens shouting joyfully 'His head is off!'

Four years later Archbishop Laud suffered the same shameful death, and the same riotous scenes followed. He was almost more hated than Strafford, and at one time his palace at Lambeth was so fiercely assailed by the London 'prentices, marching thither to the beat of a drum, that he was obliged to mount cannon upon the battlements for its defence.

Six months after the execution of Strafford, Parliament drew up a Grand Remonstrance in which an obvious attempt was made to shift the balance of power from the Crown to the Commons. There was a majority of only eleven in an assembly of three hundred members, but among the eleven was a red-faced squire from Huntingdonshire, Oliver Cromwell by name.

Great excitement was caused in London by the King's attempt on January 4th, 1642, personally to impeach five Puritan members of Parliament who had incurred his displeasure. Followed by his Gentlemen-Pensioners and some hundreds of armed courtiers and officers, he entered the House of Commons and demanded the immediate surrender of Hampden, Pym, Holles, Hazelrigg and Strode. But, as he himself observed, 'the birds had flown'; they had bolted for shelter to a house in Coleman Street, Cripplegate. One of the Queen's own ladies had warned Pym in time, and Charles had no choice but to withdraw. No English sovereign has ever set foot in the House of Commons since that day.

The sequel to Charles's impetuous action was peculiar. The Commons adjourned till January 11th, but in the meanwhile set up a permanent Committee at the Grocers' Hall, within the City boundaries whither they thought the King would hardly dare to follow them. They were wrong.

The next day His Majesty announced that he would dine with the Sheriffs in Guildhall. Rigid and stern he sat in his State coach, while the mob pressed round him with repeated cries of 'Privilege of Parliament!' Stiffly and coldly he demanded that the Lord Mayor and Aldermen should seek out and deliver up the five Members who had taken refuge in their midst. And it must have been very stiffly and coldly that he dined with a small company of City worthies, for he realized that no attempt would be made to meet his wishes.

Knowing now that war was inevitable, he soon removed his wife and children first to Hampton Court and then to Windsor, before he himself went to raise the royal standard at Nottingham. He was never to enter London again except as a prisoner on his way to trial and execution.

During the seven years that followed the parliamentarians held the capital and the great seaports. London was the largest taxable area in the realm; it contained the accumulated wealth of the richest community in Europe: it controlled the Customs Offices and the chief printing presses; it paid and commanded the by-now-efficient militia known as the Trained Bands. Even if the whole population was not unanimous in supporting those who strove against the King there was no man who did not fear that if the Royalists should storm the City plunder and destruction would follow. The most strenuous preparations were therefore made to ward off and defeat any attack.

No battle of the Civil War ever raged nearer to London than Turnham Green. When the Royalists, under the command of the King's dashing young nephew, Prince Rupert, marched eastward from Brentford they found an army twice as large as their own barring the way to the City.

Here is the story in the words of a contemporary, Bulstrode Whitelocke:

The City Bands marched forth very cheerfully, under the command of Major General Skippon, who made short and encouraging speeches to his soldiers—'Come, my boys, my brave boys, let us pray heartily and fight heartily—remember the cause is for God.' Beyond Hammersmith, in a lane, were placed the great guns, ready to be drawn up as there should be occasion, and a little beyond that were the carriages, in a field close to the highway.

The General, Lord Essex, rode from regiment to regiment encouraging them, and when he had spoken to them the soldiers would throw up their caps and cry, 'Hey for old Robin!'

A Lady Mayoress of the time of Charles the First

Her dress shows the transition between Elizabethan and Cucolean fashions, but is as yet untouched by Puritan severity

Engraving by Wenceslas Hollar

The City goodwives, and others mindful of their husbands and friends, sent many cartloads of wines, and provisions, and good things, to Turnham Green, with which the soldiers were refreshed and made merry; and the more when they heard that the King and all his army had retreated.

Turnham Green is still an open space; there are flower-beds to make it gay, and cricket is played there in summer; but if any deep digging has to be done people sometimes find human bones, swords, steel caps, and other relics of the memorable day when the tide of Civil War rose to within eight miles of St. Paul's.

London contributed 20,000 men to Cromwell's invincible New Model Army, and many a young linen-draper donned a scarlet cloak, a buff jerkin and a steel cap, and learned to fight on horseback and on foot with broadsword and with musket. The City was spared the horrors of sack and pillage; but for eleven years she was packed with troops, ruthless, rough-mannered troops. For the first time in its long history this proud and powerful community had to learn to live under an absolute despotism such as no Plantagenet, Tudor or Stuart had ever attempted to set up.

In the once-merry month of May poor old King James's *Book of Sports* was publicly burnt by the hangman. Maypoles were chopped up for firewood, playhouses and beargardens were closed. It was soon as dangerous to hang up a sprig of holly at Christmas as it was to possess a copy of the Book of Common Prayer. The one game to which little objection seems to have been made was nine pins, which the Cromwellian soldiers played so noisily and so late at night in the aisles of St. Paul's Cathedral that decent citizens in the neighbourhood could not sleep.

The Royalist defeat at Naseby in June, 1645, was celebrated by a banquet in the Grocers' Hall attended by Members of both Houses of Parliament. They little thought how soon their power would be broken, and all pretence of parliamentary government thrown overboard.

On the morrow of this banquet the Common Council was called upon to consider what should be done with the 3,000 unfortunate Cavalier prisoners of war then herded together in the south cloister of St. Paul's. What decision was reached has not been put on record. Humanity to a defeated foe was not a characteristic of the Puritan nature: there was no warrant for it in the Old Testament. These prisoners may have been left to die of privation; or they may have been sold as slaves on the Gold Coast, as were the Scottish captives after the Battle of Worcester five years later.

London had not resisted King Charles and his Archbishop only to submit meekly to Cromwell and his buff-coated legions. She told Parliament that she had her own views on church reform, wanted full control of her own Trained Bands, and desired that the Army should be abolished. Nobody paid any heed: and the City Companies were soon compelled to sell their plate to maintain the Army which Parliament itself had now begun to fear.

Meanwhile the fortunes of King Charles and his friends were going steadily from bad to worse: and then in the grey January days of 1649 the people of London knew that they had only to betake themselves to Westminster in order to see the King on his way to and from Westminster Hall to be tried for his life on the impossible charge that he had 'maliciously levied war against the present Parliament and the people therein represented'.

All the approaches to the Hall were lined by carefully-chosen troopers, who spat upon the King as he passed, blew tobacco smoke in his face, and kept up a monotonous bellowing of 'Justice! Execution!' But above their clamour he could hear far off, faint, quickly-stifled cries of 'God Save Your Majesty!' Cromwell could not trust the Londoners to show no pity for Charles: he dared not let them draw too near that sorrowful, unflinching, black-clad figure.

Presently those who ventured again into Whitehall heard the hollow sound of hammers upon planks as workmen began to erect a scaffold, surrounded by a high black-draped railing, outside the Banqueting Hall. When on that scaffold the last scene of the tragedy was enacted spectators perched on roof-tops and clung to chimneys; none of them would ever forget the deep groan of horror which arose when the masked executioner held high the severed head of the King.

For three or four years London, like the rest of the realm, was at the mercy of the fifty-six petty tyrants composing

An early example of a 'News-Letter'

Parliament in session: the speaker in his chair; two clerks ready to take notes

the Rump Parliament. When in 1653 Cromwell set them packing he dubbed himself the Lord Protector and called his new Republic the Commonwealth; but words could not mask the fact that he was a dictator. The old cry 'Privilege of Parliament' was out of date now, and the dark-browed royal exile whom the Puritans called 'the Young Man Charles Stuart' had been twice defeated in desperate attempts to win back his heritage. It seemed as if 'jack-boot rule' had come to stay.

However little large numbers of Londoners may have

liked life under a dictatorship, the merchants soon realized that Cromwell's bold foreign policy was paying dividends. The capture of the island of Jamaica gave them a fresh source both of sugar and of negro slave-labour, and they perceived the importance of having a new Continental foothold at Dunkerque. It was the younger people and the more gently-nurtured among their elders who on the one hand fretted at the general gloom and on the other looked back wistfully to the days that perhaps seemed happier than they really were. Then a time came when Royalists and Republicans were of one mind—and that was when it appeared that Cromwell thought of proclaiming himself King. Many merchants were also displeased when the Lord Protector introduced a colony of Jews from Amsterdam, allowed them to build a synagogue, and granted them certain commercial privileges which the London community regarded as excessive.

King Charles, living shabbily and anxiously in the Netherlands, was cheered by secret and confidential reports that Royalist sympathizers were growing bolder and more numerous every day; and presently refugees from England began to seek him out, runaway London 'prentices among them. News came of an attempt upon the Lord Protector's life. Someone left a basket containing a firework near his apartments in Whitehall; but it failed to explode, and he was fated to die in his bed, on a night of great storm and high wind.

Mr. John Evelyn, a loyal though not a warlike Royalist, wrote in his diary his impressions of Oliver Cromwell's funeral. He described how the body was borne from Somerset House to Westminster Abbey in a velvet-covered 'bed of state' drawn by six horses. On this lay a life-size effigy in royal robes, with 'crown, sceptre and globe like a king'; heralds followed, wearing their tabards: then a led horse, its housings, 'embroidered all over in gold': but, concluded Mr. Evelyn,

it was the joyfullest funerall ever I saw, for there was none that cried but dogs, which the soldiers hooted away with a barbarious noise, drinking and taking tobacco in the streets as they went.

London was actively involved in many of the events leading up to the Restoration of Charles the Second only seven months later. The Army was now supreme, for Richard Cromwell, the Protector's son, otherwise 'Tumble-down Dick', showed no readiness to take over the authority which had been formally bequeathed to him by his father. But it was an Army without a head, unless one counted General Monck, who was in command of the Common-wealth forces in Scotland: and presently it became known that he was marching south, a rough, resolute man, whose real purpose no one could fathom. It was said, however, that his wife, a masterful woman, desired a royalist Restoration.

Three months after Cromwell's death the 'prentices of London were shouting for a Free Parliament, and pelting with old slippers, turnip-tops, stones and tiles the soldiers sent to silence them. Young clerks drank secret healths to 'Somebody', and though the name of Charles Stuart was seldom spoken, the thought of him was in every heart. Recruits flocked to Monck's army, even though he had not yet plainly declared the object of his southward march. He reached London in February, he and his officers wearing red and white favours in their hats, trumpeters going before. Meanwhile the City of London had decided to pay no more taxes until a Free Parliament were assembled, and that miserable set of puppets called the 'Rump' ordered Monck to march into the City and pull down the gates and port-cullises there.

This, wrote Mr. Evelyn, 'exceedingly exasperated the

Cittie'. But perceiving 'how wretched a pack of knaves would have taken away his commission', and repenting of what he had done to the 'Cittie', Monck marched with his Army to Whitehall, dissolved the Rump, and summoned the Old (or Long) Parliament—what remained of it. The next day he marched back to the City, watched by silent,

Listening to an open-air sermon at Paul's Cross

The Puritans made great use of the pulpit as an instrument of propaganda, and Londoners were not daunted by the length of the five-hour-long discourses

From a contemporary print

uneasy multitudes. At Guildhall he formally informed the Lord Mayor and Aldermen what he had done. He also expressed his regret that he had obeyed the Rump so far as to do injury to 'that famous city which of all ages has been the bulwark of Parliament and general liberty'. Astonished and delighted, the Mayor and Common Council drank his health, invited him to dinner, ordered the bells of the City to be rung, and bonfires to be lighted in the streets.

After the execution of Charles the First his statue outside the Royal Exchange was cast down and over the empty niche was inscribed in Latin 'The Tyrant is gone, the last of the Kings'. On March 15th, 1660, just before the Exchange closed, a man came with a ladder and a pot of paint, climbed up, and blotted out the inscription. He then threw up his cap and cried, 'God bless King Charles the Second!' In this cry the 'whole Exchange joined with the greatest shout'.

On May 29th, when the sky was blue and the hawthorns were in flower, the King reached the capital where citizens of all classes were tumbling over each other to greet him. The Army, helpless now, stood in rigid, sullen ranks on Blackheath, listening to the bells of the morris-dancers and the music of pipe and tabor, and watching the Lord Mayor waiting at the head of some 120,000 people to welcome the royal wanderer home.

The procession passed slowly through the City, to the sound of carillons, cheers and martial music, the King patiently and smilingly bowing right and left, his high-crowned hat with its deep red feather in his hand more often than upon his head. It passed so slowly that it was not until nine o'clock that he was able to dismount before his Palace of Whitehall. Tapestry hung from the windows through one of which his father had stepped forth onto the scaffold eleven years before.

CHAPTER IX

Plague, Fire and 'Popery'

WHEN 'the King enjoyed his own again', and new maypoles were set up, and morris-bells were heard once more, and playhouses re-opened, London was still the straggling, complicated City of Plantagenet and Tudor days. For six miles—if we include Westminster—it extended along the northern bank of the Thames, where the watermen were now more numerous, and more audacious, and more noisy than ever. A great wave of gaiety and loyalty swept over the people, and though certain Puritan sects still made themselves troublesome, they were a small minority, and the majority dealt harshly by them. Parliament, the City, the whole country, would have launched a campaign of ruthless retribution if they had had their will. Even the dead were not spared. Londoners gathered in their hundreds to see the bodies of Cromwell, Ireton and other Puritan leaders swinging from gibbets at Tyburn. Only one man seems to have kept his head, and that was the man who had suffered most during the evil times that had just ended—the King himself. He was as merciful as his subjects would allow him to be.

Twenty-eight of the surviving regicides were tried for their lives, but London had the satisfaction of seeing only ten of them executed. When their fate was being discussed at the royal council-board in Whitehall the King scribbled a note and pushed it across to the Lord Chancellor, Sir Edward

Hyde,[1] 'I confess', he wrote, 'I am weary of hanging. Let it sleep.'

The Londoners had many opportunities of seeing for themselves their tall, dark-browed, ugly, yet likeable monarch.

'New maypoles were set up and morris-bells were heard once more'

A typical London scene near the church of St. Andrew Undershaft

He dined in public every weekday, and the galleries of the Banqueting Hall at Whitehall were thronged by interested spectators. On Sundays, his loyal subjects (as many as of them as could squeeze into the Chapel Royal, St. James's) saw him at Church—and sometimes saw him fall tranquilly asleep if the sermon were very lengthy or very dull. They

[1] Afterwards Earl of Clarendon.

were able to watch him feeding his ducks on the lakeside in St. James's Park, where he also kept antelopes, goats, an elk and some Arabian sheep.

It is related that on one occasion when the Lord Mayor of London arrived at Court to deliver a message from the City to His Majesty, he found the King, hat in hand, busily throwing corn to the wildfowl on the lake. His Worship, also, of course, hat in hand, hesitated. Etiquette forbade that he should deliver his message to a hatless sovereign.

'If,' he said, 'If your Majesty would please to be covered'—

'Oh,' answered the King, cheerfully, 'You may deliver your message, my Lord Mayor—it is to the ducks that I take off my hat.'

His encounters with the Chief Magistrate were often rather comical: for example, when at a Guildhall banquet in the year 1676 Sir Robert Viner, being more than a little tipsy, became so uproariously familiar that the King tried to slip away towards his waiting coach; but Sir Robert followed him, 'and catching him fast by the hand cried out, with a vehement oath, "Sir, you shall stay and take t'other bottle".' The merry monarch looked kindly at him over his shoulder, and with a smile repeated the line of the old song,

He that is drunk is as great as a King;

after which he allowed himself to be led back to the high table.

Mr. Samuel Pepys, Clerk of the Acts to the Navy, was a keen observer of the great tides of life and action flowing through the London streets, and his diary is a much livelier chronicle than that kept by his serious-minded friend, Mr. John Evelyn. Nobody knew better than Mr. Pepys how constant an interest the King and his brother, James, Duke of York, took in naval affairs, but it is to Mr. Evelyn that we owe a delightful glimpse of the two royal brothers racing their yachts from Greenwich to Gravesend for a wager of £100. Evelyn was aboard the King's yacht and noted that His Majesty steered her for part of the course with his own hands. After the race, which ended in a draw, the diarist dined with the King.

He must have felt greatly flattered when the conversation turned upon his book, *Fumifugium*, a treatise on the smoke nuisance in London, then daily growing more intolerable. In the dedication to the King Mr. Evelyn had described how one day when he was walking in the Palace of Whitehall 'a presumptuous smoake did so invade the Court that all the rooms, galleries and places about it were filled and infested with it'. The fumes from a brew-house near the Palace produced such a 'horrid cloud' that to anyone coming up the river the City appeared 'like a sea where no land was within ken'. Indoors the 'smoake', he said, 'diffused and spread a yellownesse' over the 'choysest pictures': out of doors it made the churches and palaces black, and withered the flowers and trees.

Evelyn's proposed remedy was to remove from the City all brewers, dyers, soap-boilers, lime-burners and other 'manifest nuisances', and to plant the low-lying lands to the east and south-west with sweet hedges of musk, rose, lavender, Spanish broom and bay. All these ideas sovereign and subject discussed as they dined aboard the royal yacht: and the King declared that he was 'resolved to have something done about it'. But nothing effective was done; and even now a great deal remains to do.

The royal yachts and barges lay constantly at anchor off the foreshore by the Palace of Whitehall, but it was not only aboard such craft that Londoners looking out upon the Thames caught sight of their King. Sometimes he would take a pair of sculls and go for a row all alone, laying aside his bushy dark periwig in hot weather, and so making him-

self less easy to recognize: sometimes he and his brother the
Duke of York would swim in the river between Battersea
and Chelsea.

On June 3rd, 1665, in a great sea fight off Lowestoft, the
English fleet under the Duke of York inflicted a heavy
defeat upon the Dutch, and London went mad with joy.
People flung furniture out of their windows to feed the
bonfires in the streets. Only four days later Mr. Pepys,
walking down Drury Lane, saw something which made
him catch his breath sharply, and forget all about the victory
which was still in every mind. He knew the Lane well.
There were taverns there, a few noble houses, a cockpit in
which the cruel but popular 'sport' of cockfighting was
carried on, and the recently-erected Theatre Royal, a favourite
haunt of his, and the scene of many frivolous and witty plays
of the kind likely to please a frivolous and witty monarch—
and his people. Actresses instead of young boys now took
the women's parts, and the scenery was as elaborate as in the
Elizabethan playhouse it had been simple.

The summer of 1665 had been exceptionally hot, following a very dry winter. The streams which had once flowed
through—and even under—the City had almost run dry;
the air was full of dust, and the dust was full of the germs of
disease. The Plague, which had not fallen upon London for
many years, was just beginning to spread. Mr. Pepys
stopped short with an exclamation of dismay when he saw
on three closely-barred oaken doors red crosses roughly
painted, and under each the words, *Lord, have mercy on us!*
He knew at once what that meant, though it was a sight he
had never seen before.

Every week it was the duty of the sextons and clerks of
the hundred and forty London parishes to draw up what
were called Bills of Mortality—lists of the deaths which had
taken place within their boundaries during that period.

When the Great Plague of 1665 was at its peak, about 1̸,̸ citizens were dying of it every day.

Such people as *could* remove themselves to the country did so without undue delay. The King, who had already planned a summer progress in the West Country, lingered till the end of July, when he went by river from Hampton Court to Greenwich to view his new buildings there and inspect a ship. He could hear the London bells tolling for the dead as he was rowed through the stricken City. It was soon the only sound to be heard in the streets, except the ghastly creak of the deathcarts and the dull clink of the iron clapper as men went to and fro among the desolate houses crying, 'Bring out your dead!' Grass sprouted between the cobblestones: and presently the river, once so gaily dotted with boats and wherries, was as lonely as a river flowing through a wilderness. The churchyards were filling up so fast that in some cases the level rose as much as ten feet. A distant flicker of torchlight after dark usually meant that more unfortunate victims were being hastily laid in shallow graves.

Among the stout-hearted few who refused to flee was Mr. Pepys. Old General Monck, too, now Duke of Albemarle, remained quietly in his lodgings in the Cockpit at Whitehall, and Lord Craven, a much older man, stuck to his house in Drury Lane and helped those who were trying to keep order at a time when law and local government seemed on the point of falling to pieces.

In September there was a meeting of magistrates held in the vestry of Greenwich Church 'in order to be doing something for the keeping of the plague from growing'. Among the cases considered was one which touched the hearts of them all. As the pestilence spread, households which had been stricken were isolated as far as might be, and the inhabitants were only allowed to creep forth for a short time after dark. People living on the outskirts of the City were strictly forbidden to receive or harbour any refugees. It happened that there lived in Gracechurch Street, a saddler and his wife who had lost all their children but one. Then in the hour of their despair a good friend of theirs came by stealth from Greenwich, took this child from them stark naked, and after putting it into fresh garments, brought it home with him. The magistrates agreed that it should be permitted to be kept in the town.

By the end of October the full force of the disease had spent itself. Merchants were gathering again to do business together, a few shops were venturing to take down their shutters; and by the end of January a hard frost had done its work, and Mr. and Mrs. Pepys dared to go to church again, where the piled-up graves in the churchyard were covered with snow.

Those 'persons of quality' who had stuck to their posts received from the King silver flagons suitably inscribed. Mr. Pepys got no flagon; but he got something better—for His Majesty came up to him, grasped him warmly by both hands, and said, 'Mr. Pepys, I do give you thanks for your good service all this year, and I assure you I am very sensible of it.'

Another ordeal lay just ahead of London—but this time the King was there, as the Londoners had good reason to know.

On September 2nd, 1666, a fire broke out in a bakehouse in Pudding Lane, near London Bridge, and, fanned by a strong east wind, spread rapidly. Almost before Londoners had time to realize what was happening their proud and ancient City was a great forest of quivering flames, over which brooded a pall of lurid smoke.

Mr. Pepys hurried to Whitehall with the news, and the King, much concerned, told him to go back to the City and command the Lord Mayor to pull down all the houses in the path of the flames—no very difficult task when so many of them were so flimsily made, and when hooks and ropes were always kept ready for the purpose. But the citizens were too anxious to remove their household goods—mostly by water —to have time to spare for the obvious counter-measures, and as for the Lord Mayor, Sir Thomas Bludworth, he proved quite unworthy of his office. Pepys met him in Cannon Street,

like a man spent, with a handkercher about his neck. To the King's message he cried, like a fainting woman, 'Lord! what can I do? The people will not obey me'—he needed no more soldiers—and for himself he must go and refresh himself, having been up all night.

In the evening the royal barge made its way down a river choked with laden shipping, for the King, unlike the Lord Mayor, was prepared to deal with the situation. And still the fire spread, making a 'horrid, malicious, bloody flame' in the sky.

What London needed was not so much soldiers as seamen, and the King saw to it that seamen were not lacking. Not only did he call out the Trained Bands to keep order; he brought seamen from the fleet and workmen from the royal dockyards to blow up the houses which the Lord Mayor could not (or would not) pull down.

All that day he was King of England, riding up and down the line of his workmen with a bag of guineas at his side, commanding, threatening, rewarding, sometimes dismounting at the fiercest points to pass the buckets with his own hands, or standing ankle deep in water, amid sparks and falling masonry, to see his orders for blowing up houses carried out.[1]

Almost before the fire had smouldered out the King was caring for the relief of the poor folk left homeless. He

[1] From *King Charles II* by Dr. Arthur Bryant.

ordered that bread from the Navy stores should be dis-
tributed among them; he himself went to Moorfields, where
thousands were huddled together, and rode up and down to
calm their fears. He then summoned his architect, Christopher
Wren, and his friend, Mr. John Evelyn, to discuss plans for
the rebuilding of the City. A Proclamation was next issued.
No more wooden houses: no more narrow, twisted lanes;
no more smoke-emitting trades to be carried on within a
certain radius; a 'fair quay' to run the whole length of the
north bank of the Thames. But the citizens would not yield
up the right to rebuild their houses on the old foundations;
and to this day you can follow the course of the narrow
medieval lanes—and even read their former quaint names
on the modern office walls—Blowbladder Lane, Bandyleg
Lane, Duck Lane.

Of the eighty-nine churches which perished in the Great
Fire Wren rebuilt fifty-two. Those which have survived
an even greater fire give us a good idea of what the rest
looked like—real City churches, full of pompous memorials
to City worthies, and each with a wrought-iron sword-rest
ready to hold the City sword if the Lord Mayor should
worship there in state. Among those of which only the spires
remained after World War II were St. Mary le Bow, the
church of the famous Bow bells broadcast by the B.B.C.
almost all over the globe, and St. Bride's, Fleet Street, the
newspapermen's own.

Sir Christopher's biggest task was the rebuilding of St.
Paul's Cathedral. His first plan was rather startling—a
circular edifice with sloping tiers of seats, but neither the
King nor his brother, James, Duke of York, approved, and
after several other schemes had been laid before them, that
was finally chosen which, translated into stone, now seems
to dominate the whole City.

From 1675 to 1710 the diminutive figure of the great

architect was constantly to be seen watching over the slow development of the cathedral; and not always at ground level, either, for as Sarah, Duchess of Marlborough, scornfully remarked, Sir Christopher was 'dragged up and down in a basket three or four times a week for £200 a year'. King Charles himself laid the base of the column on the west side of the north entrance to the new Royal Exchange. He arrived escorted by kettledrums and trumpets and gave twenty pounds in gold to the workmen. When Wren was rebuilding St. Stephen's, Walbrook, the Churchwardens gave twenty guineas to his wife to 'incuridg and hast' him in the work.

London, like the greater part of England, was aggressively and anxiously Protestant. The Londoners welcomed with relief the passing of the Test Act in 1673, which prevented anyone not a member of the Anglican Church from holding any office of state. By this Act the Admiralty was deprived of one of the best administrators the Navy had ever had, James, Duke of York; but as a Roman Catholic he was hated and feared by the people. And he was the next heir to the throne.

There now appeared upon the scene the two precious rascals named Titus Oates and Israel Tonge. Between them they had worked out a bright scheme by which they could destroy the whole Catholic community in England and at the same time win substantial rewards for their public-spirited conduct. Oates, a weird-looking creature with a huge flat face, appeared before the Privy Council, and was keenly questioned by Charles, who at once saw through the imposture: but the public were quite ready to believe in a far-reaching Catholic plot to murder the King, massacre the Londoners, burn London again to the ground, impose the Pope's authority at the point of the sword, and establish the Duke of York as King. If anyone doubted whether such people were capable of such wickedness they had only to go and read for themselves the inscription on the Monument erected the year before to commemorate the Great Fire of 1666. This said that the 'dreadful burning of this Protestant City had been begun and carried on by the treachery and malice of the Popish faction—in order to introduce Popery and slavery'. If once, why not twice?

Titus Oates had sworn to the truth of his story before a London merchant and magistrate, Sir Edmund Berry Godfrey, a nervous, melancholy man. Five days later Sir Edmund's body was discovered in a ditch on Primrose Hill, pierced by his own sword and with marks of strangulation round the neck. The real murderers were probably Oates and Tonge, who thus provided the necessary 'evidence' of their trustworthiness.

London went mad. The body of Sir Edmund was paraded through the streets by the mob: medals were struck, some suggested by the supposed escape of the King, others by the undoubted death of poor Sir Edmund. Here you see the monarch walking peacefully along with his dog while a man with a gun takes aim at him from behind a tree; there you see the head of the magistrate with two mysterious hands tightening a scarf round his throat.

Even the King could do little to protect—much less save—the innocent victims of this abominable plot. There was a reign of terror lasting nearly two years. To Charles, now secretly a member of the same faith, it must have been unspeakably painful; and also, considering that Parliament kept him very short of money, he must have grudged the pension of £480 a year awarded to Oates for his imaginary services to the Crown. But alone of all the Stuarts he understood the English people and knew just how far he dared resist their will. He did not, as he said, want to 'go on his travels again': so he put his scruples in his pocket and kept them there.

The London mob were devoted to the King's son, the young Duke of Monmouth, whose mother, Lucy Walter, declared that she had been lawfully married to his father at Rotterdam in 1649. He was good-looking, he was a stout Protestant, and many Londoners were hotly in favour of Lord Shaftesbury's endeavours to have him recognized as the next heir to the throne, passing over the unpopular Duke of York. When his lordship stood his trial for high treason

Medal struck to commemorate the alleged 'Popish Plott'

A conspirator aiming his gun at the King, who is quietly taking his dog for a walk

Original in British Museum

at the Old Bailey in 1681, the populace surged into the court-room, howled down the Judges, and afterwards stoned the witnesses for the prosecution all the way along the Strand. When the jury, in defiance of the evidence, refused to convict him, bonfires were kindled into which effigies of Popes, Cardinals and devils were flung, and any passer-by who would not drink Lord Shaftesbury's health in wine might find himself forced to drink it in water—from the gutter.

After a time common sense returned. Oates ceased to seem a heroic figure. The King was better loved than ever.

Crowds watched him every day setting out on his morning walk, and he never failed to answer their blessings with a few gracious words, though he also strode along at such a pace that any claimants or petitioners for royal favours were soon outstripped. At the height of the Popish terror he had stoutly defended the Queen against Oates's monstrous charge that she was trying to poison the husband she dearly loved: and when in 1683 the man accused the Duke of York of treason, Charles felt that the time had come for action. A fine of £100,000, which, of course, he could not pay, checked Oates's career and landed him in prison. After the accession of James the Second he was rightly convicted of perjury, and sentenced to be flogged, to stand in the pillory five times a year, and to be imprisoned for life. One does not hear of any Londoners attempting to rescue him from the pillory outside the Royal Exchange, or uttering any words of pity when he was whipped through the streets from Aldgate to Newgate.

At the end of January, 1685, Londoners were crowding into the City churches at all hours of the day and on all days of the week to pray that King Charles might recover from the illness which had laid him low. Better kings have seldom been loved so well. For the past three or four years he had done what neither Plantagenet, nor Tudor, nor any other Stuart but himself had been able to do for long; he had governed the country without a Parliament—an experiment which had cost his father his crown but which he carried out with astonishing success. His people realized now that he wished them well, and, in his own way, had served them well. When he died London lamented him bitterly.

Although the new King's religion was a matter for regret, he was known to be honest, active, and patriotic. He had two Protestant daughters, one married to a Dutch and one to a Danish Prince. All his children by his second wife,

Mary Beatrice of Modena, had died in infancy. So things went on quietly enough for a time.

The Lord Mayor's Show of 1686 seems to have been planned with an eye to the new King's well-known love of the sea; one of the huge, cumbersome chariots showed

Seal of James, Duke of York (James the Second)
as Lord High Admiral

The Navy has had few more able and faithful servants, ashore or afloat

Original in British Museum

Neptune seated on a dolphin and surrounded by mermaids and tritons. But the real temper of the City was revealed by the fact that the new Lord Mayor, Sir John Shorter, was a Dissenter; 'a very odd, ignorant person', commented Mr. Evelyn. With characteristic tactlessness James brought with him to the Guildhall banquet an Italian priest representing the Pope; and within those same ancient walls the Lords

Spiritual and Temporal would draw up a declaration of allegiance to the King's Dutch son-in-law only two years later.

During those years the people of London were angered and alarmed by the sight of numerous priests and monks walking boldly in the streets where by a still unrepealed law they had no right to be seen. The inscription on the Monument, ascribing to the Catholics the disaster it commemorated, was erased; and anyone who wished to see the sovereign at his devotions had his nose offended by the fumes of incense and his ears by the sound of Latin chants. None the less the news of Monmouth's landing at Lyme Regis in June, 1685, had been received with mixed feelings, for his 'army' consisted of a rabble of miners and labourers who might confidently be expected to loot London, if they ever got there. In spite of the one-time popularity of the 'Protestant Duke', James's stern suppression of the pitiful rebellion seems to have contented the City well enough. It was otherwise when he began to reorganize the Army, to publish on his own authority Declarations of Indulgence granting general liberty of conscience, and—another alarming thing—to show that by living within his income he intended to make himself financially independent of Parliament.

The first Declaration of Indulgence was received in the City with some degree of approval, for Dissenters as well as Roman Catholics were included; but the second was another matter, and the London clergy almost to a man disobeyed the royal command that it should be read aloud from every pulpit. It was the same all over the country; and when the Archbishop of Canterbury and six other Bishops intervened the King clapped them into the Tower to await their trial for 'sedition and incitement to rebellion'. Two days later guns were thundering to announce the birth of a son to James and his Queen, a son who, if he survived, would bar the way to the confidently-awaited Protestant succession.

The trial of the Bishops was held in Westminster Hall on June 29th, and it is an interesting fact that the Jury was drawn not from London in particular but from Middlesex in general. The result was a triumphant acquittal. As the stout-hearted prelates passed on their way from the Hall, Londoners were kneeling to beg their blessing, and that night the sky over the City was flickering with the light of bon-fires, while the bells of the City churches rang a merry peal.

For some time past Louis the Fourteenth of France had been warning his cousin James that William of Orange was massing troops and ships for an invasion of England. This warning the English King could hardly credit; but when seven English noblemen formally invited the Dutch Prince to come with his English-born wife and take possession of the throne, William was prepared for prompt action. Caring nothing for England, he cared much for his own country, and English blood and gold would soon be poured forth to aid Holland in her struggle against France.

London soon learned that he had landed at Torbay; then came the news that the King's army had melted away on Salisbury Plain: and finally the King himself, haggard yet hopeful, appeared at Whitehall. His few remaining friends persuaded him first to send his wife and baby son to France, and then to make arrangements to follow them. All was not lost while he was still alive, but his anxiety to summon a Parliament met with no encouragement in London.

That James should flee was Dutch William's own wish. The presence of his father-in-law in London was most awkward. Who could tell how popular feeling might change? He was therefore much annoyed when a gang of priest-hunting Kentish fishermen boarded the small vessel upon which James was about to set sail and, mistaking his long, pale face for that of his hated Jesuit confessor, Father

Petre, brought him by force back to land. Such of the Privy Council as were sitting in London sent an escort to bring the fugitive home: and then the thing happened which William and his friends most feared. The temper of the Londoners suddenly changed. 'Gentlemen and citizens on horseback' streamed out to Blackheath to meet James, and when his coach came into view 'two eminent merchants' rode up and begged him to continue his way through the City, instead of proceeding by barge to Lambeth as had been intended. He must have thought he was dreaming when the people cheered and the bells rang. Many followed him as far as Whitehall, even to the door of his bedroom, making it, as he said himself, 'look more like a day of triumph than humiliation'.

Dutch William having refused an invitation to come to London for a personal interview, on the plea that he could not enter the City while it contained any troops not under his command, the King hopefully suggested to the Common Council that he should place himself under its protection for the time being. But the Common Council declined to undertake a responsibility which it might not be able to fulfil. Sudden waves of popular emotion could not now check, much less change, the march of events. James agreed that his own Guards, whom he could no longer trust, should be replaced by Dutch troops, and their heavy tramp was heard in Whitehall as they took up their positions round the Palace. Next day he was curtly informed that 'for the greater quiet of the City and the greater safety of his person' he must remove himself thence by noon on the morrow. A few days later he was on his way to France. And so London got what many Londoners had long desired—a Protestant King. Yellow ribbons blossomed on all sides. And in some buttonholes miniature warming-pans appeared, to show that the wearer believed—or pretended to believe—the ridiculous story that the royal baby had been an impostor introduced into the Palace hidden in that seventeenth-century equivalent of a hot-water bottle.

The Lord Mayor and Aldermen, with fifty other citizens of London were invited to join members of both Houses at St. James's Palace to discuss with William what should next be done. Bad weather delayed the return of Mary to her native England, so it was only William who sat listening silently and attentively to their deliberations—a meagre, sickly man, with the beak of a bird of prey. In due course it was agreed that he and his wife should reign jointly; but in the meantime the wildest scenes of destruction had occurred in and around the City, when the houses and property of many innocent people were burned and plundered merely because they were known—or suspected—to be of the same faith as the King whom the same multitude had been hailing with cheers not long before.

Most of the mob were, as a writer of the period put it, 'villainous thieves and common rogues', but among them were London 'prentices who, not content with marching down the Strand 'with oranges upon their sticks', helped to loot the Spanish Ambassador's house, to rob a 'widowed gentlewoman' of a trunk containing £500, and to perform many other violent deeds. Not until irreparable damage had been done were the Trained Bands called out to restore order; and then one of their marksmen, taking aim at a particularly noisy group of 'prentices, unluckily shot his own officer in the back.

CHAPTER X

New Habits, New Dreams, New Ideas

ONE day in the year 1659 a Londoner noted that there was now a Turkish drink to be sold in every street called Coffee, and another kind of drink called Tea, and also a drink called Chocolate—'a very hearty drink'.

The first and third of these new-fangled beverages rapidly became so popular that special Coffee Houses and Chocolate Houses were opened, and throve exceedingly. Tea, less liked at first, was drunk at home.

An early Coffee House was the Rainbow in Fleet Street, much patronized by the young barristers from the Inns of Court. Local vintners, resenting competition, tried to have it closed down, and neighbours objected to the constant smell of roasting coffee-berries. But coffee had come to stay. 'Now', wrote one regretful rhymester,

Now, alas, this drink has credit got
And he's no gentleman that drinks it not.

The new drinks were for a long time beyond the reach of the less prosperous Londoners. Good tea cost as much as fifty shillings a pound, and chocolate and coffee almost as much. Early in the reign of William and Mary a certain John Houghton was selling all three at his shop in Bartholomew Lane; also brandy, soap-balls, spectacles, onions, jointed dolls and a variety of other things. In addition he printed a weekly pamphlet for the benefit of curates, gardeners, schoolmasters and cookmaids seeking employment, one of the earliest examples of the 'small ad' on record.

The Coffee House was a convenient meeting place for men of similar interests and occupations. Politicians and poets, lawyers and merchants each had their favourite haunts. The name of 'Lloyds', famous through the world as the centre of the marine insurance business, commemorates the Coffee House where in the last years of the seventeenth century people used to gather to discuss that business. Here is a typical day in the life of a London citizen in the year 1706.

He rose at five; worked in his Counting House till eight, then breakfasted on toast and Cheshire cheese. After serving in his own shop for two hours, he went round to a neighbouring Coffee House for news; shop again until he 'dined' at twelve noon in his residence over the shop, the principal dish being 'a thundering joint'. At one o'clock he was to be seen 'on Change', otherwise 'at the Stock Exchange'; at three he went to Lloyds, 'on business'; back to the shop for an hour, then 'for recreation' round to yet another Coffee House. Thence he went to a tavern, drank a glass or two of sack with acquaintances, and so home to a light supper and early bed. He had donned his night-cap and drawn the curtains of his 'four-poster' before the great bell of Bow Church tolled nine. The wives of these coffee-drinking merchants became more and more addicted to tea, in imitation of tall, handsome Queen Mary, her stout, amiable sister, Princess Anne, and all the noble ladies in the land. The East India Company imported not only tea and coffee but also delicate Chinese porcelain tea-pots, coffee-pots, cups and saucers. When the London silversmiths added tea-spoons and sugar-tongs, cream-jugs and sugar-basins, the tea-table became a very pretty sight indeed.

Unfortunately the poorer part of the population had also discovered a new drink, cheap, indeed, but far from wholesome. This was the coarse gin known as 'Hollands', which was exported in huge quantities from the Dutch distilleries with the full approval of Dutch William.

Every London merchant no longer lived over his office, warehouse or shop. Largely under pressure from their would-be-modish womankind many of them were moving outwards to Soho and Bloomsbury, where the fine new houses were scarcely touched by City grime. Nor did the 'prentice lodge with his master unless in the smaller and

Great Seal of William and Mary

In him London got what many Londoners had long desired—a Protestant King. He and his Queen were financially associated with the foundation of the Bank of England, but his wars against France cost the City dear

humbler households. The lad of Tudor times, a sturdy, sometimes rowdy fellow, with his flat woollen cap and his formidable wooden club, had vanished. Country gentlemen no longer sent their sons to seek their fortune in the City, which may be the reason why in Georgian days the City Fathers were notorious for their imperfect table-manners. The traditional turtle-soup at the annual banquet was greedily, and no doubt noisily, ladled into the mouth, and fingers were used instead of forks when eating poultry or game. What of the poor 'prentice boy who had now little hope of ever becoming a Lord Mayor? He was the starveling pauper child, handed over with a sum of £5 to any employer willing to take him off the hands of the Parish, and his prospects of living to man's estate were not bright.

Among the topics discussed in the Coffee Houses during the years 1693–94 was the foundation of the Bank of England. Planned by a Scotsman to provide funds for the Continental campaigns of a Dutchman, it was not at first conspicuously English. Parliament hesitated over granting the necessary Charter, and the City was hardly less doubtful. Some people said that it was a Dutch idea, and that they had 'too many Dutch things already'; others feared it might make the Throne independent of Parliament. King William contributed £10,000: so did Queen Mary; and among the original subscribers were the Dutch-born Court painter, Sir Godfrey Kneller, and that fine old sea-dog, Sir Cloudesley Shovel, whose ship was lost off the Scilly Isles in 1707.

It was not until 1724 that the Bank was established in Threadneedle Street, near the Royal Exchange—a site where it remains to this day. The original clerks, recruited from among haberdashers, cheesemongers and menservants, received a commencing salary of £50 a year, and worked for twelve or thirteen hours every day except Sunday. No special training or previous experience was demanded. The applicant had to write a good hand and 'cast up accounts'; the rest he learned as he went along.

Members of the Board sat on large green cushions with bowls of sweet-smelling flowers before them. The Chairman kept order with the aid of a hammer and a handbell.

After the death of Queen Mary in 1694 Londoners saw less than ever of their Dutch King. The smoke and fog of the City were bad for his asthma, and he lived chiefly at

Hampton Court, where he added a whole new wing in the style of Versailles, and Kensington, when he built himself a palace in the Dutch manner. London did not love him. Too much English blood was being shed, too much English gold was being spent in the interminable wars between Holland and France. But when after the death of James the Second, the French king, Louis the Fourteenth, acknowledged the young Prince of Wales as 'James the Third', the temper of England changed. She did not want a half-Italian Roman Catholic king; and long after King William had been laid beside his faithful Queen in the Stuart vault at Westminster prayers were offered up that their successor, Queen Anne, might be a joyful mother of children. A mother she had been, many times, but only once a joyful mother, and then her joy soon turned to mourning, for William, Duke of Gloucester, her only child to survive babyhood, followed his little brothers and sisters into that vault in 1700, at the early age of eleven.

A year later the succession was settled by Act of Parliament upon the Electress Sophia of Hanover, granddaughter of James the First and Sixth, and her descendants.

Londoners were fond of Queen Anne and did not dislike her plain, homely consort, Prince George of Denmark. They knew that she was good, if not clever. Lame and unwieldy though she was, they liked to see her carried into St. Paul's Cathedral in a sort of open sedan chair to render thanks to God for the great victories won against Louis the Fourteenth by the first English General of supreme military genius, John Churchill, Duke of Marlborough. Blenheim, Ramillies, Oudenarde, Malplaquet. The merchants in the Coffee Houses rolled these outlandish names upon their tongues with growing satisfaction.

The cobbled streets were noisier than ever, for more wheeled vehicles were used, coaches richly painted and gilded, clattering hackney-coaches, thundering drays. Hawkers, men, women and children, cried their wares at the top of their voices—'lily-white vinegar', tame birds, water from the New River, parsnips, cherries, oysters, eels, sealing-wax, mops and brooms, posies of country flowers, 'delicate cow-cumbers'. It will be remembered that the parents of Sally

Great Seal of Queen Anne

Londoners were fond of Queen Anne—they knew that she was good, if not clever. She came often to St. Paul's to return thanks for Marlborough's victories

British Museum

who lived 'in our Alley' were street-traders, one selling cabbage-nets and the other

> *laces long to such as care to buy 'em.*

Foot passengers hugged the wall in wet weather to avoid the spurts of mud thrown up by the passing traffic. Your only hope was to hail a coach or a chairman. Dean Swift in his famous description of a City shower suggests that a young lawyer from the Temple might sometimes to save his face pretend to hail a coach he could not really afford to hire.

To shops in crowds the draggled females fly,
Pretend to cheapen goods but nothing buy.
The Templar spruce while every spout's abroach
Stays till 'tis fair but seems to call a coach.
The tucked-up sempstress walks with hasty strides
While streams roll down her oiled umbrella's sides.
Here various kinds by various fortunes led
Commence acquaintance underneath a shed.
Triumphant Tories and desponding Whigs
Forget their feuds and join to save their wigs.

At that time only women carried umbrellas. A man named Jonas Hanway who was a baby when Queen Anne died would be laughed at some forty years later when he boldly appeared in the streets of London sheltering his three-cornered hat under one of these despised objects.

It is to John Gay, the author of the *Beggar's Opera*, that we owe many of the most vivid pictures of London under Queen Anne and George the First. With him we can walk through the noisy City, see the signboards swinging, combs and stockings dangling on strings outside shops, maids twirling mops out of windows, bulls being led to the bull-ring, fiddlers and drummers collecting outside any house where a wedding feast is in progress.

It was perilous to stir abroad alone on a moonless night, even though householders were compelled on such nights to hang out candles in lanthorns until 11 p.m. Footpads, known as 'Mohocks', were always on the prowl, and a prudent straggler, especially if he knew himself to be not quite sober, would engage a link-boy to escort him home. Outside many old houses in London you may still see the heavy iron extinguishers in which links were quenched. Oil lamps were not set up in the streets till 1736, and gas-lighting was not introduced until 1807. Against the 'Mohocks' the old night-watchmen, familiarly called

'Charlies', could do very little, and, indeed, did not try to do much.

When it became clear that poor, good Queen Anne's life was drawing to a close the City was shaken with rumours and honeycombed with plots. Nobody knew better than she that the rightful heir to the throne was her half-brother,

Brackets for oil lamps and extinguishers for links

Outside a house (*now demolished*) in Berkeley Square

called by the Jacobites 'James the Third'; but she could do little to right the wrong done in 1688, and when she died the pro-Hanoverian party hastened to proclaim George, Elector of Hanover, as King George the First of England. But for this haste the whole course of English history would have been different.

Soon crowds assembled to see—if not to salute—their new King, a swarthy, unsmiling man who could speak no word of English. With him he brought two German ladies, one so tall that the Londoners dubbed her 'the Maypole' and one so stout that she was unkindly called 'the Elephant'. His Queen, the unhappy Sophia Dorothea of Zell, he kept captive in the lonely fortress of Ahlden. Of these things the citizens did not approve. When they gathered booing and hissing round 'the Maypole's great gilded coach she shouted in her heavy German accent. 'But we only kom for all your coots,' meaning 'for the good of you all'. 'Yes,' called out a quick-witted Cockney, 'All our goods—and our chattels, too!'

The new Royal Family attended a service of thanksgiving in St. Paul's. Wren's cathedral was practically complete and the architect, now eighty-six years of age, had naturally expected to receive some marks of honour from the House of Hanover. Far from it. Without a word of apology or explanation, he was dismissed from the post of Surveyor of Public Works which he had held for forty-nine years and was quite fit to hold a little longer. Once a year until his death in 1723 the tiny wizened old gentleman in the large unfashionable wig was brought up to London by easy stages so that he might look once more upon the great dome, the stately arches and the lofty columns created by his genius. Having looked, he went quietly back to his house at Hampton, then a comparatively remote and rural retreat.

When George the First paid his first state visit to the City the Lady Mayoress, wife of Sir William Humphreys, confidently expected that he would kiss her cheek, a custom observed by Charles the Second and James the Second, and even by William the Third, but allowed to lapse under Queen Anne. She appeared in a long-trained gown of rich black velvet, carrying an enormous bouquet of flowers and followed by two small pages. When she perceived that neither the King, nor his dumpy, red-cheeked son, the Prince of Wales, nor his stately daughter-in-law, Caroline of Anspach, would bestow the traditional kiss, she swept angrily away, shouting to one page to hold up her train and to the other to carry her 'bucket' for her.

There was a great flutter in London when news came in December, 1715, that James Francis Edward, the Stuart claimant to the throne, had landed in Scotland, and that a number of Jacobite noblemen were rallying round him, but the rising fizzled out, and in January, 1716, six of these noblemen were tried for High Treason in Westminster Hall. As many Londoners as could squeeze into the Hall watched the proceedings, and many more gathered on Tower Hill to see sentence of death executed upon Lord Derwentwater and Lord Kenmare. Two nights before, some loiterer near the Tower must have passed a closely-muffled 'woman' stealing away in the darkness but nobody guessed that 'she' was a third Scottish Lord, Lord Nithsdale, whom his heroic wife had smuggled out of his dungeon in disguise.

Persons about to be publicly beheaded usually wore the deepest mourning upon that occasion. Just before laying his head on the block Lord Kenmare observed, 'I had so little thought of dying so soon I have not provided a black suit. I am sorry for this. I might otherwise have died with more decency.' The crowd heard these words; they heard him pray aloud for his 'rightful sovereign, King James'; and they saw him give a handful of golden guineas to the executioner.

There was no public sympathy with the cause for which these Scots had risked their lives and all they possessed, but with them personally there was a great deal. Four of the six were reprieved, but the City of London did not welcome the Venetian Ambassador's suggestion that any Jacobites willing to fight for Venice against the Turks should be allowed to go and do so. Trade between London and Turkey had never been more flourishing; and did not the best coffee come from the Levant?

The English government remained uneasy; and when, on May 29th, the anniversary of Charles the Second's joyful Restoration, certain soldiers observed the old custom of

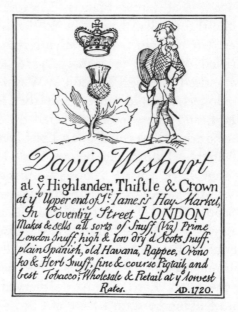

Trade card of a London Tobacconist, 1720

It was in London that the passion for tobacco and snuff reached its greatest heights during the Georgian period

wearing sprigs of oak,[1] two of them were flogged almost to death in Hyde Park.

From the point of view of the City the outstanding chapter in the reign of George the First was the financial crash known as the South Sea Bubble. It began in Queen Anne's time, when the ill-fated Mississipi Company was at the peak of its prosperity in France. In 1711 the South Sea Company

---

[1] In memory of the tree at Boscobel where the fugitive King hid from his foes.

was formed, with a capital of ten million pounds invested in Government stock. To this company was later assigned the privilege, granted by Spain under the Treaty of Utrecht, of sending one merchantman each year to the Spanish possessions in Central and South America, and of supplying African slaves to the settlers there. At first all went well— too well. The price of shares soared. Speculators invested every penny upon which they could lay their hands, and not even the outbreak of war with Spain in 1718 daunted them. In January, 1720, Parliament agreed that the Company should take over the whole of the National Debt ($£30,000,000$) on being guaranteed 5 per cent a year for a term of seven and a half years. A wild scramble followed. Great ladies sold their jewels, great lords mortgaged their estates, rich merchants turned their securities into cash, Jew and Gentile, wise and foolish, all drugged by the same wild dream, crowded into 'Change Alley' and bought up every share.

At the beginning of August, 1720, the Bubble was glowing over London like a huge, rainbow-tinted moon. Stock stood at the impossible figure of 1,000 per cent. The King himself was said to love the South Sea Company as much as he loved the Duchess of Kendal, otherwise Madame de Schulenberg, otherwise 'the Maypole', one of his two hated German favourites. The poet Gay, having been given some shares, refused to sell out, even though a sensible friend urged him to sell at least enough to obtain an income of $£100$ a year and thus make himself sure of a 'clean shirt and a leg of mutton every day'.

There was one man of letters who escaped the fever. This was Dean Swift, who wrote,

> There is a gulf where thousands fell,
> Here all the bold adventurers came;
> A narrow sound, though deep as hell,
> 'Change Alley is the dreadful name.

Subscribers here by thousands float,
    And jostle one another down,
Each paddling in his leaky boat,
    And here they fish for gold—and drown.

The headquarters of the Company were at South Sea House, an imposing building on the corner of Threadneedle Street and Bishopsgate Street. Nearly a hundred years later Charles Lamb described it standing derelict. Great maps of Mexico and Peru hung dusty and cracking on the discoloured walls; fire-buckets were still ranged in rows as they had been when fire would have been a great danger to the supposedly valuable documents in the vaults below—documents which did not even exist.

In July, 1720, the Mississipi scheme crashed. Two months later South Sea shares had lost half their value and were still falling. The directors of the Bank of England, who had never approved of either wild enterprise, shook their full-bottomed wigs gloomily. In December, when panic was rising even faster than the shares fell, Parliament ordered a full investigation. Follies, irregularities, and worse things came to light. It was found that the Chancellor of the Exchequer and other Government officials had accepted bribes. The Treasurer of the Company and several of the directors fled. It was also found that the vaults beneath South Sea House were not, after all, stuffed with securities. And so the Bubble burst, leaving a wide area of ruin and despair.

Some of the directors were compelled to forfeit all their profits for the relief of those most hardly hit; some of the shareholders, Sir Robert Walpole the Prime Minister among them, had cleverly sold out in time, and were the richer for the rest of their lives. The country as a whole was poorer for many years, but England was more fortunate than France, where the havoc caused by the collapse of the

Mississipi scheme marked a long step towards the Revolution.

London was, however, in no chastened mood. Sir Robert's pacific policy did not chime with her aggressive attitude, which was reinforced when it became known that these hated Spaniards had torn off the ear of a Jamaica skipper

Citizens of the reign of Queen Anne, George the First and George the Second

Showing the changes in fashion which marked the first half of the eighteenth century

From prints of the period

named Jenkins. Popular clamour forced the Government to embark upon what came to be known as the War of Jenkins' Ear. Bell-ringing and bonfires greeted the news. 'They are ringing their bells now,' remarked the Prime Minister, grimly. 'Presently they will be wringing their hands.'

Then in 1742 Londoners had *another* war to discuss when they met in taverns and Coffee Houses or on 'Change. This was the War of the Austrian Succession, which George the

Second regarded as threatening the security of his dominions in Hanover. The King himself led his Anglo-German forces to victory at the Battle of Dettingen a year later, but the London steeples were not often shaken by joyful peals during the years that followed. 'Our army', wrote Horace Walpole, Sir Robert's elegant youngest son, 'is running away—all that is left of it to run.'

Ten days after that letter was written, young Charles Edward whom the Jacobites called the 'Prince of Wales' landed on the island of Eriskay to claim the crown for his father whom they called 'James the Third'.

At first London heard this news with surprise—even with amusement. Nobody was alarmed. France was too busy with the War of the Austrian Succession to make this romantic escapade an excuse for a large-scale attack on her old enemy, England. She lent a frigate to carry the young Prince to Eriskay; more she would not do.

Horace Walpole, snug in his little red brick house in Arlington Street, Piccadilly, was inclined to mock at 'the Boy', as he called him. Then word came that the Highland clans were furbishing up their antiquated swords and shields and flocking to enroll themselves under the standard which Charles Edward had set up in Glen Finnan. The supposed 'savages' proceeded to capture Edinburgh and though the English red-coats still held out on the Castle Rock, the Prince held feast in his ancestors' Palace of Holyrood, and his badge, the white cockade, was to be seen on all sides.

There followed the defeat of the English General, Sir John Cope, at Prestonpans, and the road to the south seemed to lie open. Mr. Walpole was then by no means the only Londoner to get into a fearful flutter. It seemed as if there would be a run on the Bank of England, from which nervous persons were withdrawing their deposits; but a number of merchants met at Garraway's Coffee House and promised

to give the Bank their support. They also opened a sub-
scription list to raise troops, some individual contributions
amounting to as much as £2,000. Household troops,
cavalry and infantry were encamped in Hyde Park, where
bugle-calls, the shrill whinnying of horses and the steady
thud of marching feet were soon to be heard. The King
hurried back from Hanover. His son, Ernest, Duke of
Cumberland, still smarting from his defeat by the French
at the Battle of Fontenoy, was despatched northward to
put down the rebellion with the greatest severity possible.

Conflicting rumours ran like wildfire through the City
while the young Prince Charles continued his march south
until he reached Derby. Mr. Walpole accused the English
Government of 'wet-brown-paperness', and declared that he
personally would 'wonderfully dislike being a loyal sufferer
in a threadbare coat and shivering in an ante-chamber at
Hanover'. The Duke of Newcastle, then at the head of the
'wet-brown-paper' Cabinet, was said to have shut himself
up for a whole day at his house[1] in Lincoln's Inn Fields considering whether he should stick to King George or change
sides and go over to King James. There really *was* a run on
the Bank, which might have had to close down if someone
had not thought of a clever plan of paying out in sixpences.

The danger of a Stuart Restoration had never been great
and was very soon over. London belfries rocked when early
in the year 1746 news came that Cumberland had re-captured
Carlisle; four months later the discipline, experience and
superior armament of the Anglo-German army proved too
much for the desperate valour of men badly equipped and
practically untrained. Gorgeous fireworks blazed and
quivered in Hyde Park when London celebrated the defeat
of young Charles at Culloden; George Frederick Handel
composed a triumphal oratorio, *Judas Maccabaeus*; and it was

[1] Still standing on the west side of the Fields.

decided to bestow the name of the 'Cumberland Gate' upon the new gate recently opened into Hyde Park near the execution place at Tyburn.

It was, however, the Londoners who dubbed the victorious Duke 'Butcher' Cumberland when they heard accounts of his ruthlessness to the defeated after Culloden. The English Government, having offered a reward of £30,000 for the capture of 'Bonnie Prince Charlie', dead or alive, confidently expected that some hungry Scot would soon claim that dazzling sum. It was never claimed. The Prince, after hiding undiscovered and unbetrayed among the poorest of his own Scottish folk, escaped to France. Tradition says that he returned to England in secret more than once between 1750 and 1760. The muffled-up 'woman' who snatched up the glove from the floor of Westminster Hall after the traditional challenge had been uttered in defence of George the Third's rights may perhaps have been 'Charles the Third' in disguise. The Church of St. Mary-le-Strand, then as now a narrow island in a roaring river of traffic, is said to have been the scene of his formal reception into the Church of England—a change which had no influence either upon his life or his luck.

In Westminster Hall, draped in their honour with scarlet cloth, a group of Jacobite lords stood their trial for High Treason. In was 1715 over again. This time it was Lord Kilmarnock instead of Lord Derwentwater whose good looks won pity for him. A sentimental lady vowed that she had made herself 'as yellow as a jonquil' grieving for him. But it was gruff, jocular, indomitable Lord Balmerino who won the hearts of the London mob. On his way back from Westminster to the Tower for execution the crowd gathered at Charing Cross saw him stop the coach and buy from a street hawker what they would have called 'gooseberries' but he called 'honey-blobs'.

A few days later Mr. Walpole passed with a slight shudder beneath Temple Bar, where the heads of the Jacobite lords were stuck up on poles to blacken and wither in the smoky London air. Spy-glasses could be hired by the curious for a penny a peep.

In the 1780's there often rolled eastward through the central arch a stately coach in which sat a little red-haired boy. It was Francis, Viscount Yarmouth (later Marquis of Hertford) on his way to watch the two giants striking the hour with their clubs on the clock-bell outside St. Dunstan's. They were his delight. He often said that when he grew to be a man he would buy them for his very own. In 1830 the churchwardens sold by auction what they regarded as a lot of old junk, and a raffish-looking, ginger-whiskered personage then bought the clock and the giants for £210. It was, of course, Lord Hertford. He set up the clock in the garden of his Regent's Park villa, where for many years the giants beat out the hours of his far-from-admirable life. Now they are back in Fleet Street, where he had loved to watch them long ago, when George the Third was King and Temple Bar still spanned the roaring street.

CHAPTER XI

A City both Grim and Gay

THE day of the illustrated newspaper and the strip-cartoon was still far distant when George the Second sat on the throne, but anyone calling at a certain house in Leicester Fields could then buy for the modest sum of one shilling sets of twelve prints each telling a complete story. The house was that of William Hogarth, painter and engraver, and the background of his pictures was almost invariably London. Among his most popular sequences was one showing the difference in character and fortune between two apprentices, Francis Goodchild and Tom Idle. Francis marries his master's daughter, is taken into partnership, and prospers mightily; Tom, after many misdeeds, is seen packed off to Newgate on a charge of murder. And, finally, the virtuous Francis becomes Lord Mayor of London.

Within the City he would walk before all other subjects of the Crown, even the Princes of the Blood Royal; he was chief magistrate of the City, perpetual coroner of London and Southwark, conservator of the River Thames and Medway, Chief Butler of England. The Lord Mayor of our own times holds all these offices. No troops may march through London without his leave; the secret pass-word of the Tower sentries is communicated to him every night; he is at once informed when a sovereign dies, he is Chief Officer of the realm until a new one is proclaimed, and he attends the first Privy Council of each reign. When a reigning monarch visits the City the Lord Mayor meets him outside the Law

Courts and proffers the City sword, which is lightly touched by a royal hand; and it is here that a crimson cord marks the City boundary when heralds come to proclaim at the Mansion House and the Royal Exchange the opening of yet another reign. Old Temple Bar, designed by Wren and

Hogarth's Industrious Apprentice at Church

Notice the 'three-decker' pulpit, the crowded galleries, the aged pew-opener
with her bunch of keys at her side, the three-cornered hats each on its peg

erected in 1672, was taken down in 1878 and removed, piece by piece, to Theobald's Park: through its archway the rich tide of London life rolled for more than two centuries and as late as 1822 a man was alive who could remember seeing the ghastly heads of criminals (or alleged criminals) stuck upon poles over the top.

Even after the slow spread of education had removed

many absurd beliefs many people who ought to have known better were easily thrown into a panic. In 1750, for example, a slight earth-tremor occurred in London; a month later a second tremor set bells jangling and crockery clashing: and after that thousands of foolish folk were convinced that only one more month would pass before the whole City was laid in ruins. Families who owned carriages streamed westward in a long procession; those who had none encamped in the parks until the scare gradually died down; and for one person who, like Horace Walpole, laughed at the whole thing, there were multitudes who trembled and believed.

A far more real peril was the pestilence known as gaol fever of which the Lord Mayor, two Judges and several members of the Jury died after a trial during the same spring season. It is as a preventive of this no-longer-existing scourge that Judges still carry bouquets on certain occasions, and a sweet-smelling posy is always set before the Judge who opens the law term at the Old Bailey.

Between 1751 and 1759 London merchants were anxiously watching the fluctuations of the wars raging between England and France in India and in America. Upon the outcome of those wars the prosperity of the City and of the whole realm would necessarily depend. With characteristic shrewdness they were quick to realize that a certain energetic ex-Cavalry-officer, William Pitt by name, who became Secretary of State in 1756 was the man best fitted to bring things to the right conclusion. They showed their confidence in him by making him a Freeman at once, without waiting for him to prove his mettle; and he had to promise at his installation that he would 'pay his scot and bear his lot'—the 'scot' being a tribute or tax, and the 'lot' that share assigned to any particular holder of the Freedom of the City. Two years later the sky over London was flickering with fireworks to celebrate victories by land and sea in Africa and India, in Canada, and on the Rhine.

Some of the sights which Londoners crowded to see were violent and cruel—the hangings at Tyburn, for example, and the grim procession from Newgate along what is now Oxford Street, when the prison chaplain sat in the cart with the condemned man, an empty coffin at their feet, and the mob showed neither pity nor horror, only a noisy, gaping curiosity. In 1760 they saw Earl Ferrers hanged for the murder of his steward. All Europe marvelled, for in no other country would a man of his rank have been condemned to death for killing a person of low degree.

The parish clerk of St. Sepulchre's Church, Holborn, used to ring a bell (still preserved in the church) and recite a set of doggerel verses outside the condemned cell on the eve of an execution. At St. Sepulchre's porch the wagon would halt so that the criminal might receive a posy of flowers, which he stuck in his buttonhole, and drink a cup of wine, which he tossed off with a defiant laugh. One of the last occasions when this old custom was observed was in 1774, at the execution of the famous highwayman, Jack Rann, nicknamed 'Sixteen-String Jack' from the bunches of many-coloured ribbons he wore at his knees. After a long career of crime he was hanged for stealing a watch and eighteen-pence from a clergyman.

When George the Third succeeded to the throne in 1760 London was able for the first time since 1685 to acclaim a King who was stoutly British in speech and feeling, whatever he may have been in blood. It was when attending his marriage to Charlotte of Mecklenburg-Strelitz that the members of the Common Council first wore robes of the fine colour called mazarine blue. They may not have realized that their predecessors wore blue gowns when they greeted Margaret of Anjou in 1445, but they might have been interested to know that their successors in the twentieth century would wear gowns of that hue.

The City Fathers had now formed the habit of expressing their opinions on matters unconnected with the Governance of the City, and of conveying such opinions to the King, often personally and always in a most dictatorial tone. George the Third did not like this at all. With rebellions and revolutions breaking out on all sides, he would have preferred not to be reminded of the 'glorious and necessary' Revolution of 1688 to which he owed his throne; and the fact that the City Fathers supported the American colonies during the War of Independence displeased him even more. His face grew redder than ever, and his stammer became more pronounced, when irrepressible Lord Mayors like William Beckford and John Wilkes lectured him boldly on his duties and responsibilities.

The subject of Beckford's expostulation was the fact that though John Wilkes had been four times elected M.P. for Middlesex, each election was declared void. Wilkes had been imprisoned in the Tower for attacking the Government in his weekly *North Briton*, but the Lord Chief Justice, on the grounds that he was a Member of Parliament, ordered his release. 'Wilkes and Liberty!' cried the London mob with enthusiasm. Even his violent squint found apologists. One woman was heard to remark that Mr. Wilkes 'certainly did squint', to which another replied, 'No more than an honest man should!' Not for twelve years was he allowed to take his seat in the House of Commons, but in the meantime he had grown comparatively tame. The ex-rebel was even elected Lord Mayor and, later, City Chamberlain. No crowds gathered when he walked abroad wearing the uniform of a Colonel of Militia, scarlet and buff, with a large cocked hat and high boots.

His personal charm must have been almost irresistible, for it overcame the prejudice of that great Londoner and good man, Dr. Samuel Johnson, who disliked Wilkes's public activities and his private character with equal vigour, and yet who observed tolerantly on one occasion, 'Jack has a great variety of talk; Jack is a scholar; Jack has the manners of a gentleman. . . . I would rather do Jack a kindness than not'.

It is a little curious to see Dr. Johnson setting himself up as a judge of manners, for his own were proverbially odd and uncouth. Though not a Londoner born, no man ever loved London better than this growling philosopher so often to be seen lumbering along his beloved Fleet Street, wearing dusty raiment and a rusty old wig, and touching each lamp-post as he went by. He once observed that a man who was tired of London was tired of life; also that he thought the full tide of existence was at Charing Cross. On Sunday he would put on clean linen and a better wig, and go to church at St. Clement Danes. He would certainly have agreed with the fashionable gentleman who preferred the smell of a flambeau in the playhouse to the scents of a country evening in May.

The four principal playhouses, Drury Lane, Covent Garden, the Haymarket and His Majesty's, must have smelt strongly of these flambeaux; also of oranges, lamp-oil, hair-powder and humanity. Dr. Johnson's friend, David Garrick, was the brightest star in the theatrical sky—a ruddy-faced little fellow with blazing dark eyes, who could make people laugh or shiver as he pleased. Of course, he acted *Macbeth*, *Richard the Third* and *Hamlet* in the costume of his own day, powdered wig, lace ruffles, buckled shoes, full-skirted brocade coat; but everyone took it for granted that he would.

Sometimes playgoers might be entertained by other 'comics' than those actually on the stage. For example, Dr. Johnson's biographer James Boswell relates how one evening, sitting with a serious Scottish parson-poet, Dr. Hugh Blair, in the pit of Drury Lane, he was suddenly seized with a wild freak of youthful extravagance, and began to imitate the lowing of a cow.

'The universal cry of the galleries was', he writes, "*Encore* the cow! *Encore* the cow!" In the pride of my heart I attempted imitations of some other animals with very inferior effect. My reverend friend, anxious for my fame, with an

David Garrick as Macbeth

Like all the actors of the time, he played Shakespearean parts in eighteenth-century costume

From a contemporary print

air of the utmost earnestness and gravity, addressed me thus; "My dear Sir, I would confine myself to the cow!"

As early as the reign of Queen Anne, and for a long time after, the purveyors of choice snuff and tobacco were frequently Scotsmen, and this fact was indicated in their trade cards and on their signboards. After 'the '45' England made it a penal offence for any Scot to wear the kilt, but when this outrageous law was repealed in 1782 images of kilted Highlanders with snuff-boxes in their hands soon began to appear

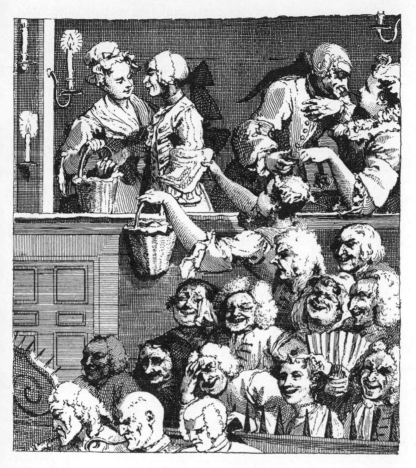

Hogarth's 'Laughing Audience'

One beau is buying oranges, another gives a pinch of snuff to a friend. Neither is as much amused as the people in the cheaper seats next to the orchestra. Notice the spikes on the partition

outside the tobacconists'.and snuff-sellers' shops. There are several of these to be seen in the London Museum and another, affectionately known as 'Phineas', is still every year the centre of a lively 'rag' between the students of University College and King's College.

In the year 1741 there was opened in London the first refuge ever provided in England for 'foundlings'—the unfortunate infants found abandoned, sometimes dying, in the streets. The sight of these poor waifs troubled the heart of Captain Thomas Coram, master mariner and shipwright, and for seventeen years he pursued his noble aim until in 1747 the great Foundling Hospital, giving shelter to six hundred children, was opened in Bloomsbury. Royal patrons and famous people rallied round. To the Chapel Handel presented a fine organ, upon which he often used to play, and to the Hospital he handed over the original score of his oratorio, *The Messiah*. Hogarth, Gainsborough and other well-known painters, either gave their pictures to be raffled or lent them for exhibition in aid of the good work. In one of these exhibitions lay the germ of the Royal Academy.

In 1926 the Governors decided to pull down the old buildings, sell the now immensely valuable site, and move the school[1] to the country.

Scenes as wild as any in London's far-from-peaceful history were witnessed in June, 1780, when Lord George Gordon, a tall, thin, half-crazy Scotsman with long red hair, raised the cry of *No Popery* and headed an unruly procession to Westminster, to demand the repeal of the Act removing certain handicaps from English Roman Catholics. How many of his followers had any idea what it was all about? Probably very few. But for five days and nights London was full of the crackle and glare of flames and the crash of broken windows. Nervous persons covered themselves with blue ribbons to proclaim that they were 'true blue' Protestants. Horace Walpole decked himself with such ribbons until, as he said, he 'looked like a May Day garland'; he also had his front door lined with plates of iron. Other perturbed Londoners chalked the words *No Popery* on the walls of their houses.

[1] It is now known as the Coram Foundation for Children.

At last the soldiers were called out; but, as their first instructions were that they should not fire on the people, red coats could do little against blue cockades. The chapels of foreign embassies were wrecked and plundered; the houses of blameless Catholics were burned to the ground—and not the houses of Catholics only. Because Lord Mansfield was regarded as being lukewarm in the 'good cause', his house in Bloomsbury Square was reduced to ashes, and his priceless collection of books and papers destroyed.

It seemed as if both the Government and the City were paralysed. In spite of its massive ancient walls, Newgate Prison was partially burned, and many of the prisoners set free. Presently of all the prisons in London only that in the Poultry still stood intact. Desperate characters, suddenly set free, mingled with the yelling throng. In vain the officer commanding the troops tried to arouse the magistrates to a sense of their duty. The Lord Mayor tremblingly refused to take any steps for the protection of life and property, and so the horrible nightmare went on.

Then the Privy Council met, and resolved that what the City would not do must be done without the City's authority. The King issued a Proclamation to his loyal subjects. At last more troops arrived—the Guards, whose very name struck fear.

This time they had orders to fire. They closed in on all sides and as the rattle of musketry grew louder the shouts of the rioters and the crackle of the flames sank down. Thirteen years later Lord George Gordon died—in Newgate, the grim prison which he and his crazy partisans had tried to burn to ashes. His long beard proclaimed, in an age when no Christian wore a beard of any length at all, that he had become a practising member of the Jewish faith.

As the eighteenth century moved on its way many outward changes were to be seen on the ancient face of London. Most of the streets were now paved with cobblestones; the lamplighter came round every evening with his ladder and his little oil-can. The river was still a great highway and also a great moving pleasure-ground for people of all classes, but as the state of the roads improved so did the volume of wheeled traffic increase. As regards the appearance of the men who thronged the streets, so many old fashions were discarded that members of the older generation still wearing powdered wigs and brocaded garments of many colours looked with amazement at their descendants, who first took to wearing their own hair unpowdered and tied on the nape of the neck with a large black bow, and then cut it short, in the 'ancient Roman manner'. The alarmed wig-makers went in procession to Parliament as early as 1764, when wigs were only beginning to go out of fashion; but at the turn of the century very few people except clergymen, Judges, and 'old fogeys' still wore the wig. Only Judges and barristers wear it today. But the most revolutionary change of all was the substitution of trousers for knee-breeches.

The Industrial Revolution, the result of the introduction of machinery and the development of steam power, did not affect London as much as it did the northern and north-western parts of England, where were congregated most of the 'dark, Satanic mills' so hated by the poet Blake; but unfortunately the living conditions of the poor continued to get worse, and there were certain London parishes, notably St. Giles-in-the-Fields, where poverty, filth and squalor brought forth in terrible abundance their wonted harvest of cruelty, disease, and crime.

Most of the comparatively few people who deplored these things proposed a remedy which the great majority of Britons were reluctant to apply—the strong physic of Revolution. Even the scenes of slaughter accompanying the French upheaval of 1789 did not at first give sufficient warning to the Left Wing English Whigs who sympathized

—quite rightly—with all the oppressed and who hailed the destruction of the Bastille as a great and glorious event. To the average Londoner the very name of that fortress-prison suggested hordes of famished captives languishing in chains; they did not know that the prisoners numbered only seven, and that their worst grievances were usually connected with the way the chicken for their dinner was cooked or the colour and cut of the garments provided for their wearing.

Soon people were flocking to the Royal Circus to see what described itself as 'One of the grandest Spectacles that ever engaged the feelings of Mankind', namely 'the Capture and Demolition of that horrid Sepulchre of People, the Bastille . . . together with the Proceedings which gave Freedom to the Empire of France'. Could historic irony go further?

The final tableau showed

Britannia in her triumphal Carr, supporting grand Transparent Portraits of the King and Queen of Great Britain.

Sober folk in London were shocked when the French King and Queen perished by the new-fangled mechanical instrument of execution called the guillotine; their horror grew when they heard of the September Massacres which drenched Paris in blood; only a few extremists were impressed by the declaration of the French Republic that 'all Governments were its enemies and all peoples were its friends'. Loyal Associations sprang up; preparations were made to defend the Tower and protect the Bank of England if similar outbreaks seemed imminent in London. When, in February 1st, 1793, France declared war, the City not only voted a loyal address to the King but offered to give a bounty of fifty shillings to every able seaman and every landsman ready to fight for his country.

Glorious British victories at sea set bells ringing in London during the first stage of the war with France. The freedom of the City was voted to the Admirals concerned, one of whom, Horatio Nelson, quickly became the idol of the populace. On November 10th, 1800, he was entertained to a banquet by the Lord Mayor; the mob unharnessed the horses from his carriage and dragged it from Ludgate Hill to Guild-hall, while ladies excitedly waved their handkerchiefs from every balcony and window. He has been described by a modern poet in these lines:

> *Look on him—empty sleeve and eye dim-cold,*
> *Faded blue coat and tarnished knightly stars,*
> *Rebellious lock of shadowing hair grey-gold,*
> *Meagre and restless body warped with scars;*

but one feels sure that on this occasion the blue coat was his best, and the knightly stars were untarnished.

In the meantime General Napoleon Bonaparte, Corsican by birth, soldier by calling, had overthrown the French Republic, and, upon the ancient Roman pattern so popular in France, had proclaimed himself First Consul. So began the long, desperate struggle between Great Britain and this amazing soldier-statesman-dictator before whom the other Great Powers of Europe went down like nine-pins.

There was a deceptive lull in 1802, when the Peace of Amiens was signed. London, hoping for a renewal of trade with the Continent, broke forth into bonfires. Large coloured pictures called 'transparencies' shimmered after dark and showed Britannia, Commerce, Peace, and other stout symbolical ladies in attitudes expressive of satisfaction. In May, 1803, Great Britain declared war on France. Two days later Nelson set off for Portsmouth to board his flagship the *Victory*. One year later Napoleon, already self-appointed First Consul for life, proclaimed himself Emperor of the French.

Meanwhile more than 20,000 volunteers had been raised in London alone. Aldermen learnt to shoulder muskets, Common Councillors studied military drill, lawyers trampled the green lawns of the Temple Bar, as they marched and counter-marched under the loud-voiced commands of veteran soldiers: and little Londoners quaked in their shoes at the threat, 'Boney will get you if you're naughty.'

The news of the great victory at Trafalgar on October 21st, 1805 was darkened for the English people by the death of Nelson. When his body lay in state in the Painted Hall at Greenwich Londoners flocked in their thousands to pay their last tribute; and when his huge, unwieldy funeral car, covered with nodding black plumes, toiled up Ludgate Hill to St. Paul's the watching multitude wept without restraint.

Pensioners from Greenwich Hospital preceded it in their blue coats and three-cornered hats; seamen and marines from the *Victory* came next, each wearing a large crepe bow; a long train of noble coaches containing the great ones of the land continued the procession; and immediately in front of the funeral car was the finest coach of all, adorned with the Royal Arms and the Prince of Wales' feathers, and containing the Prince of Wales in person, a tall, stout, handsome man who held a black-edged handkerchief to his eyes.

The victory of Trafalgar made invasion seem, to say the least of it, improbable. The City presently began to change its opinions about the terrible 'Boney' who, now Emperor of the French and dictator of almost all Europe, in 1806 declared the Island of Britain to be in a state of blockade. This meant that all trade was cut off between Great Britain and practically the whole Continent of Europe, a deadly blow at a nation to whom such trade was the very blood of life.

England retorted with the famous 'Orders in Council' under which France in her turn was blockaded, and neutral merchant-vessels, if they desired to trade with her, had first to unload their cargoes at some British port and, after paying certain dues, re-ship them. These Orders made and kept England supreme at sea during the perilous years when Napoleon was all but supreme on land; but they caused heavy loss and constant vexation to English merchants and manufacturers, and it was perhaps natural that the City of London should incline towards the Whig policy of 'appeasement'.

Nobody could then foresee that when a hook-nosed Anglo-Irish officer took command of the British forces in the Spanish Peninsula in 1809 that event marked the first stage in a war destined to bring Napoleon's great, sprawling Empire clattering to the ground. The name of that officer was Arthur Wellesley. After the victory of Talavera he was created Viscount Wellington; six years later a dukedom rewarded his remarkable services to the nation.

From the first the English government had confidence in Wellington; but the Common Council of London had none. In an address to King George the Third the City Fathers clamoured for the recall of a General whom they roundly accused of ignorance and incapacity. These amateur strategists also considered that the Peninsular campaign should be abandoned, little recking that Napoleon would afterwards speak of it as the 'Spanish ulcer' which drained the life-blood from his Empire.

Five years later the Lord Mayor, Aldermen, Sheriffs and Liverymen proceeded in full state to Carlton House to present a dutiful and loyal address to the Prince Regent congratulating him on

the increased prospect which recent events had afforded of the complete deliverance of Europe from a yoke most disgraceful, galling and oppressive.

They incidentally described Wellington as one whose

deeds would 'exist in the pages of history to the latest period of time'. Scarcely a year had gone since those same worthies passed no fewer than twelve resolutions demanding the dismissal of the Tory Government then in power, which, unlike the Whigs, was determined to prosecute with unflagging energy the war against Napoleon and all for which he stood. Even so did their Plantagenet predecessors clamour for the removal of 'royal counsellors' who failed to please them.

In the interim poor old King George the Third had become hopelessly mad, and his eldest son as Prince Regent had incurred the violent hatred of the City because he had abandoned his former Whig friends in order to support the Tories—and, incidentally, Wellington. So unpopular was he, so great were the groaning and hissing which greeted his public appearances, he dared not pay his annual visit to the Royal Academy to dine with the members and admire the exhibition. And when the Tsar Alexander and the King of Prussia came to London in 1814 for the victory celebrations he had to listen ruefully to his own subjects cheering two sovereigns much less humane and enlightened than himself.

It was a marvellous summer. Balloons ascended, fireworks soared, there was a mock naval battle on the Serpentine and a fair in St. James's Park. Wellington was the hero of the hour. Over the little booths in the Park streamed flags each bearing a huge 'W' in silver foil. At Carlton House, the Prince's residence, that letter appeared in sparkling cut glass draped with pink and white muslin.

The City entertained the illustrious foreigners to a great banquet in Guildhall, but the Lord Mayor stood behind their chairs instead of sitting with them at table. He may have been consoled by the Prince Regent's remark that this was 'the most beautiful and elegant spectacle he had ever seen!'

All these rejoicings, these pageants and processions and illuminations, were premature. London, like the rest of England, was stunned when word came in March, 1815, that Napoleon had escaped from Elba, had landed in France, and with a steadily swelling army of veterans was marching on Paris. Three months later Wellington's decisive victory at Waterloo ended Napoleon's power for mischief. The decorations were brought out again, fresh fireworks appeared as if by magic, and people felt with reason that *this* time the ogre was knocked out for good. Even the charity children were permitted to rejoice. Hundreds of them marched to St. Paul's to the Thanksgiving Service. It is pleasant to remember that they also had a service of their own every year on the Thursday before Easter. William Blake watched them once, and wrote,

> *'Twas on a Holy Thursday, their innocent faces clean,*
> *Came children walking two-by-two in red and blue and green;*
> *Grey-headed beadles walked before, with wands as white as snow,*
> *Till into the grey dome of Paul's they like Thames' waters flow.*

During the years immediately following Waterloo the Common Council was kept very busy passing resolutions and presenting addresses. They expressed their opinions on a variety of subjects, some of them, as usual, quite unconnected with the governance of the City; they expostulated, they scolded, they laid down the law. Sometimes they had the more agreeable task of offering congratulations, as when the Regent's golden-haired daughter, Princess Charlotte, was married to the dark, good-looking young Prince Leopold of Saxe-Coburg. 'A man of wax', the Londoners called him; it was the highest term of praise they knew. Waxwork shows were popular even before the celebrated Madame Tussaud opened hers in 1802. A certain Mrs. Salmon ran an exhibition in what was once 'Prince Henry's house' in Fleet Street, and advertised it outside with a large gilded salmon. Inside you could contemplate a sleeping shepherdess, a Beefeater, and the whole Royal Family, and as you departed a figure of Mother Shipton sitting by the door gave you a sharp kick with her buckled shoe.

London draped herself in black cloth when Princess Charlotte died in November, 1817. It was even said that St. Paul's had turned black as a sign of grief. Four or five years later Londoners were going out in large numbers to Kensington on the chance of seeing on the sward behind the Palace the chubby child who would one day be Queen Victoria.

CHAPTER XII

The Changing Shape of Things

A mighty mass of brick and smoke and shipping,
   Dirty and dusky but as wide as eye
Could reach, with here and there a sail just skipping
   In sight, then lost amidst the forestry
Of masts; a wilderness of steeples peeping
      On tiptoe through their sea-coal canopy;
A huge, dun cupola, like foolscap crown
On a fool's head—and that is London Town.

THE 'foolscap crown' was, of course, the dome of St. Paul's, and the poet who wrote that gloomy description of his native city was Lord Byron. Wordsworth was more fortunate. He saw a clear, cloudless day breaking over Westminster Bridge, and wrote:

Earth has not anything to show more fair;
   Dull would he be of soul who could pass by
   A sight so touching in its majesty:
   The City now doth like a garment wear
The beauty of the morning; silent, bare,
   Ships, towers, domes, theatres and temples lie
Open unto the fields and to the sky,
All bright and glittering in the smokeless air.
   Never did sun more beautifully steep
      In his first splendour valley, rock or hill;
Ne'er saw I, never felt, a calm so deep.
   The river glideth at his own sweet will,
Dear God, the very houses seem asleep
      And all that mighty heart is lying still.

Wordsworth, a countryman born and bred and a fervent lover of his own Cumberland crags and dales, was not as a rule very sensitive to the peculiar fascination of London: but in the Seventh Book of *The Prelude* he gives us some vivid glimpses of the City, as he had imagined it and afterwards remembered it. Even in far-off Cumberland and in the quiet walks of St. John's College, Cambridge, he had heard of the famous pleasure gardens at Ranelagh and Vauxhall, of the noble bridges spanning the Thames now at several points, of Gog and Magog, the gigantic Guildhall heroes said to have fought in defence of this island when Brut[1] and his Trojans overran it.

> *Vauxhall and Ranelagh! I then had heard*
> *Of your green groves and wilderness of lamps*
> *Dimming the stars, and fireworks magical,*
> *And gorgeous ladies under splendid domes,*
> *Floating in dance or warbling high in air*
> *The songs of spirits! Nor had Fancy fed*
> *With less delight upon that other class*
> *Of marvels, broad-day wonders permanent;*
> *The river proudly bridged; the dizzy top*
> *And whispering gallery of St. Paul's, the tombs*
> *Of Westminster, the giants of Guildhall.*

At that time Old London Bridge was still standing, though only a battered relic of its former self. The last mouldering remains of what had once been one of the glories of the City were carted away in 1832, a year after the jolly old sailor King, William the Fourth, had opened new London Bridge, 100 feet west of the old. Westminster Bridge, on which Wordsworth conceived his famous sonnet, was erected in the middle of the eighteenth century, in spite of energetic

---

[1] See Chapter III. The carven giants seen by Wordsworth were among the casualties of World War II; but fresh images, quite as large and not less alarming and grotesque, have recently (1953) been set up in Guildhall.

protests from the Thames watermen, who saw their prosperity imperilled; Blackfriars Bridge, intended as a public memorial to that truly great man, William Pitt, Earl of Chatham, dated from 1769. Much to the indignation of Dr. Johnson, who disliked all Scots on principle, this last Bridge was planned by Robert Mylne, whose family had been master-masons to the Kings of Scotland for five hundred years. Another Scot, James Rennie, was responsible for both

Opening of London Bridge, 1831

Small wherries and splendid barges make the river as busy as a City street. This was the sort of pageant London loved

From a contemporary engraving

the new London Bridge and the beautifully graceful Waterloo Bridge, opened by the Prince Regent in the presence of the Duke of Wellington on Waterloo Day, 1817, amid great fluttering of flags and banging of artillery. Of all these bridges in existence in the first quarter of the nineteenth century there is none now that has not been either re-built or enlarged: and the coming of the railways necessitated the construction of special bridges to carry the new form of traffic.

Before he died in 1850 Wordsworth had travelled by train at the giddy speed of twenty miles an hour. He may even have seen in 1828 the first clumsy attempt at a horseless vehicle propelled by steam: it did not prove popular, and when the first railway-line from London to Greenwich was opened in 1839 bands of music played at the stations to attract the public to the new-fangled method of travel.

Wordsworth, in spite of his natural solemnity of character, found some amusement in the open-air shows and the odd-looking people in the London streets: Punch and Judy, dancing dogs, Savoyard minstrels, Cockney ballad-singers, and other strange sights:

> The begging scavenger with hat in hand,
> The Italian, as he threads his way with care
> Steadying, far-seen, a tray of images
> Upon his head; with basket at his breast
> The Jew; the stately and slow-moving Turk
> With freight of slippers piled beneath his arm.

The Prelude was completed in 1805, two years before Londoners were startled to see Pall Mall lit by a new illuminant—coal gas; but even when lamps and candles gave all the light there was after dusk the poet was much impressed by the glow and glitter of the capital.

In spite of the solemn warnings of the well-known scientist, Sir Humphrey Davy, more and more streets were lit with gas, until by the year 1823 practically the whole of London was thus illumined. Sir Humphrey had believed that 'a mound of earth as large as Primrose Hill' would be needed to 'weigh down the gasometers'; but his fears were proved groundless, and the lamplighter no longer had to carry round his cumbersome oil-can.

Charles Lamb, as passionate a lover of London as Dr. Johnson, rejoiced to see the ever brighter shop-windows, which remained bright until eight or nine o'clock in the evening. He confessed that on Sundays he felt a gloom which was 'like a weight in the air'. 'I miss', he wrote, 'the cheer-ful cries of London, the music and the ballad-singers, the buzz and stirring murmur of the streets. Those eternal bells depress me. The closed shops repel me. Prints, pictures, and all the glittering and endless succession of knacks and gew-gaws, and ostentatiously displayed wares of trades-men . . . are shut out. No bookstalls deliciously to idle over, no busy faces to recreate the idle man who contemplates them ever passing by.'

Himself a clerk in the East India House for thirty-three years, he knew what it was to be imprisoned among those captives of commerce, cooped in 'light-excluding, pent-up offices where candles for one half the year supplied the place of the sun's light'. No gas for *them*, those pallid, dingily-clad gentlemen, each with his quill pen stuck behind his right ear when not busy in his right hand; no eight-hour-day, no Saturday half-holiday, no convenient bus to take him home to his modest abode in Hackney, Islington or Pentonville.

The introduction of gas-lighting in the streets did not reduce the annual volume of crime in the City. In 1828 this was 'unparalleled in any other civilized country'. The armed patrols, known as the Bow Street runners, or, on account of their red waistcoats, the 'Robin Redbreasts', introduced by Sir John Fielding, the novelist-magistrate at Bow Street in 1749, had done something to make highway robbery more dangerous to the robber than it had formerly been: but, strange to relate, the City, in the name of its 'rights and liberties' angrily opposed every form of organized police. That very great man, William Pitt the Younger, turned his attention to the matter in 1785; but in vain. His was a 'voice crying in the wilderness', and want, ignorance and crime continued their hideous dance of death.

In 1822 another Tory Minister, Sir Robert Peel this time,

appointed a committee to consider the rising tide of crime, and again the City opposed and obstructed. Many people were still nervous, remembering the Secret Police of France during the period of the Revolution and of the Napoleonic Empire. When in 1828 the persevering Peel returned to the

A Policeman in top hat, blue coat and white trousers

A street scene in the background, with washing hanging out. The delinquent, though youthful, looks quite a desperate character

From 'Punch': 1849

attack he was able to secure the support of his political opponents, the Whig Party, only by excluding the area of the City from the operations of his new police force, which came into being a year later. It was not until 1839 that the City, impressed by the success of Peel's plan, moved into line, but even then its police force differed (as it still does) in some respects from the Metropolitan Police, being answerable to the civic authorities instead of to a Commissioner appointed by the Home Secretary of the day, and wearing a different type of helmet. Neither force wore helmets before the year 1864. When the first thousand Metropolitan police paraded for the first time in September, 1829, they were wearing blue swallow-tail coats, white duck trousers, and black top-hats lined with leather. Their earliest nicknames reflected the general hostility. 'Blue Devils' they were dubbed, or 'Raw Lobsters'; but as time passed and they proved their worth they came to be called, in memory of Sir Robert Peel, 'Bobbies' or 'Peelers'.

They were undeniably useful during the tumults which gathered round the passing of the Reform Bill on June 7th, 1832. In modern eyes that Bill appears entirely reasonable and moderate, but there were many old-fashioned people to whom it seemed to promise nothing less than a Revolution on the French model. Poor old King William the Fourth gave the royal assent with tears, declaring that he felt his crown tottering upon his head; and when his Queen, the inoffensive Adelaide, was driving down Regent Street amid a blaze of joyful illuminations an excited mob ran beside her, bellowing 'Reform for Ever!' and, as a lady recorded who was with her, 'waving their greasy hats into her carriage'.

Another person who had deep misgivings about the Reform Bill was the Duke of Wellington. When it was seen that the windows of his London home, Apsley House, remained dark upon the night that the Bill became law the mob broke them. Perhaps they did not realize—let us hope that they did not—one of the reasons for that lack of light. The Duchess was lying dead in one of those great apartments on the ground floor, surrounded by the magnificent works of art presented to the Duke by the sovereigns and the states saved by him from the domination of Napoleon.

When he died in 1852 the streets were thronged with mourning Londoners as his funeral procession moved slowly to St. Paul's.

Alfred Tennyson the Poet Laureate wrote:

> *Hush! the Dead March wails in the people's ears;*
> *The dark crowd moves and there are sobs and tears. . . .*
> *He is gone, who seemed so great—*
> *Gone; but nothing can bereave him*
> *Of the force he made his own.*

The summer of 1832 was memorable for another reason besides the passing of the Reform Bill. There was an outbreak of Asiatic cholera in London during which more than five thousand people died. Like the Black Death, it had come from the East; and, again like the Black Death, its spread was aided by the insanitary conditions under which many wretched people lived. Hundreds of families were herded underground, in cellars where often the oozings from cesspools dripped over their heads.

In 1849 and again in 1853 the dreaded plague reappeared. The third visitation was marked by an astonishing sight—nothing less than a rich and elegant lady tending with her own hands the poorest women-victims from the maze of mean streets round about Soho. Her name was to ring through Europe only a year later: it was Florence Nightingale.

Long after piped water was made available many people preferred the old wells and springs. There was one in the stable-yard of Chesterfield House, the home of the Duke of Abercorn, and thither long queues came, jug in hand, to obtain supplies until, having had the water analysed, he had the well hastily sealed up and bricked over.

In 1858 Disraeli introduced a Bill proposing that Parliament should levy a special rate upon the metropolitan area in order to raise money to purify the Thames and complete a system of main sewers beneath the City. His opponents laughed at him for his interest in 'drain-pipes', but the Bill became law, and in 1874 £5,000,000 had been expended upon the 1,300 miles of sewers which resulted in an incalculable improvement in public health and well-being.

In the meantime a new age had set its seal upon London and upon the whole land—a progressive, earnest, prosperous, rather pompous age, the age of Queen Victoria. She was now a portly matron, but there were many people still living who remembered the slender, self-possessed eighteen-year-old girl who had succeeded her uncle, the Sailor King, in 1837.

On June 20th of that year the Lord Mayor, taking his place among the Privy Councillors at the declaration always made by a sovereign on the first day of a new reign, had shared in the general admiration felt for the grace, composure and dignity of the young Queen. You can see in the London Museum the very dress she wore on that historic occasion; the black silk is now a rusty brown, but the enormous balloon-shaped sleeves, the small waist, and the long, rather narrow skirt give quite a good idea of how she looked in the eyes of the Lord Mayor as he knelt to kiss her hand.

Londoners had frequent opportunities of seeing their diminutive but dignified young Queen during the early years of her reign, not only on state occasions such as her Coronation, her marriage to her handsome, serious-minded cousin, Prince Albert of Saxe-Coburg, her processions to open Parliament, but also when she went driving in the parks, in a royal landau when the red and white may filled the air with sweetness, or, when snow was on the ground, in a jingling horse-sleigh with Prince Albert holding the reins.

London was changing. Classical ideas, introduced by two brilliant Scottish architects, Robert and John Adam, during the second half of the previous century, were more popular

than ever. A triumphal arch in the Roman manner con-
fronted an 'Ionic screen' of Greek design at Hyde Park
Corner: colonnades and pillars rose on all sides. When,
however, the ancient Houses of Parliament were burned to
the ground in 1834 they were replaced by the group of

London street scene in the 'sixties

*The tattered but cheeky crossing-sweeper offers his arm to the crinolined
old lady, whose top-hatted page-boy is much amused. Note the omnibus
on the right with the conductor precariously perched at the rear*

From 'Punch's Almanac', 1862

buildings we see today, planned on traditional lines as a
sort of younger sister to the Abbey of Westminster just over
the way.

More than twenty years were to pass before ladies in wide
crinolines and gentlemen in tall stovepipe hats crowded to
see the machinery of a great clock arriving in a wagon
drawn by sixteen magnificent grey horses. Sir Benjamin
Hall, the First Commissioner of Works, was the godfather

of 'Big Ben', destined to become the most famous clock in the world.

All these changes in the face of London happened so gradually that people hardly perceived them. For roughly the first half of Queen Victoria's long reign her capital was the City of Charles Dickens's novels, murky and yet colourful, cruel and yet comical, a patchwork of old and new, half-timbered, lattice-windowed houses standing shoulder to shoulder with stucco and·plate glass, and haunted by odd figures that might almost have come straight out of a print by Hogarth. Though not a Londoner by birth, Dickens knew every corner of his London, from the rat-infested arches at Hungerford where little David Copperfield wept as he washed bottles to the demure and gracious red brick squares where the same David began a legal career not fated to be followed very far. In the immortal novels we meet Londoners of many kinds, sinister like Fagan, Sikes and Crook, witty like Sam Weller, horrible like Quilp, broadly funny like Mrs. Gamp, benevolent like Mr. Pickwick. Dickens makes you smell the thick yellow fog and hear the din of the streets where iron-bound wheels clattered over the uneven cobblestones by night as well as by day.

In 1834 a novelty appeared—a neat, light, two-wheeled vehicle called after its inventor a 'Hansom cab'. Drawn by sure-footed horses with bells on their harness, these cabs spanked merrily along, and their clip-clop, jingle-jangle was one of the most cheerful and characteristic sounds in the London streets right up to the end of Queen Victoria's reign and well into the reign of her son, Edward the Seventh.

The first omnibus began to run from Paddington to the City in July, 1829. It was introduced by a certain George Shillibeer and was a handsome vehicle with roses painted on the sides. It was not until 1850 that narrow seats were planted on the top. By the time that horse-buses ceased to ply (1911) wood-block paving and rubber tyres had arrived and the deafening roar of the traffic was thereby muted a little.

In the summer of 1851 Londoners of every degree had a new and wonderful experience which they owed to the

Londoners at the Great Exhibition

Top-hatted policemen to the right and left. In the foreground, an un-lucky visitor (perhaps from the country) who has had his pocket picked

From 'Punch', 1851

enterprise and imagination of Albert, the Prince Consort. This was the Great Exhibition where the nations of the world could meet for the first time not in hostility or suspicion but to reveal to each other the products of their national arts, crafts, and manufactures.

The Prince had to fight hard to get his scheme adopted. Timid people feared that the Exhibition would attract to

London all the ruffians and revolutionaries in Europe; pious people thought it savoured of worldliness; cautious people were convinced that it would prove a costly failure from a financial point of view. But the Prince went doggedly on; and he had his reward when the vast palace of glass, designed by the Duke of Devonshire's gardener, Joseph Paxton, was opened in state by the Queen herself—'the most *beautiful*, and *imposing* and *touching* spectacle ever seen', as she declared.

The ceremony also was imposing. The Queen, flushed and smiling with excitement, wore a gown of rose-coloured silk, the Prince Consort had donned the uniform of a Field-Marshal. Their eldest son and daughter were there, too, the Prince of Wales (afterwards Edward the Seventh) wearing Highland costume, the Princess Royal (later Empress of Germany), a white frock, with a garland of rosebuds in her hair. Massed choirs sang the Hallelujah Chorus. The aged Duke of Wellington, too deaf now to hear the music he had formerly loved so much, walked in the procession and afterwards examined with interest the almost overwhelming number of exhibits, ranging from the Koh-i-Noor diamond to a Canadian birch-bark canoe, from a cream-ladle shaped like a buttercup to a large machine for threshing corn, from a fountain of scented soap to a life-sized statue of a slave-girl.

The frequent admiring pauses of the Archbishop of Canterbury had an awkward result. When he paused, his chaplains immediately behind him paused also; and the Lords in Waiting, who came next *walking backwards*, were brought so often into collision with the chaplains that they all of them had very sore heels when the procession was over.

The Great Exhibition gave to Londoners of the working classes something they had never had before—an opportunity to enjoy a family jaunt that they would remember all their lives. Of the 6,201,856 people who flocked to Hyde Park that golden summer a very large number came from the poorer districts. They came in cheerful groups, grand-parents, parents, children, even babies in arms. Some of them brought well-filled baskets, in which meat pies and bottled porter figured largely; but those who preferred to buy their refreshments on the spot ate 311,731 pounds of Bath buns and 460,657 pounds of the plainer variety.

Children from orphanages and even from poor-house schools were conducted to view the wonders; one hopes they were also allowed to partake of the buns.

A year later the 'Crystal Palace' was removed, piece by piece, and re-erected at Sydenham, where for eighty-four years its concert hall, its recreation grounds, its gardens dotted with figures of prehistoric monsters and its various sideshows were a source of pleasure to thousands of people. Then one night in November, 1936, there was a strange, fierce glow in the sky to the south-east. It came from the fire which was then destroying the last visible relics of the Prince Consort's great achievement. After that no child could ever again be taken to the upper window of some London house on high ground and shown a far-off, fascinating glitter in the haze, and told that *that* was the Crystal Palace.

The profits of the Great Exhibition were used for the erection of fine public buildings, including the Victoria and Albert Museum and the Albert Hall; and the Prince Consort's part in the enterprise is commemorated in the Albert Memorial, an elaborate construction of marble, bronze, mosaic and coloured stones which it took twenty years to produce. In its hand his more-than-life-size statue holds the catalogue of the Exhibition not—as is often supposed—a copy of the Bible.

After the Prince's death in 1861 the people of London saw their Queen more and more seldom, and a completely base-less impression was spread abroad that in her grief she was neglecting her duties as a sovereign. Why did she not abdicate, and let her bluff, bearded eldest son, the Prince of Wales, take over? Everybody knew him by sight. His love of sport appealed to the Londoners, except the more serious-minded among them, who also deplored his fondness for gambling; but his beautiful Danish Princess kept to the end of her days the love of the nation, which she won at her first coming as a crinolined and ringleted young bride.

Queen Victoria, deeply hurt and much affronted, carried on steadily, and as time passed she began to emerge from her long seclusion and to taste again the sweetness of popularity. London welcomed her back with enthusiasm.

As was frequently observed at the accession of Queen Elizabeth the Second, we have 'done well under Queens'. The age of Victoria showed it yet again. In the matter of transport alone London saw amazing developments. Apart from the great main-line stations, trains began to seek their termini underground. When the first underground railway was opened amid scenes of huge excitement in 1863, timid persons prophesied that all the tunnels would collapse and bury all the travellers; but the whiskered gentlemen knew better who sat waving their top-hats in the unroofed trucks that made the trial trip.

Bicycles of the first perilous 'penny farthing' type, with a very large front wheel and a very small back one, began to appear in the streets in the late 1870's, and by 1890 Daisy Bell's 'bicycle built for two' was a familiar sight as well as being the theme of a popular song. In 1896 Parliament repealed the law compelling a man to carry a red flag in front of any mechanically-propelled vehicle moving at the rate of more than four miles an hour. Four years later the Prince of Wales bought a 6 h.p. Daimler, and by the time he became King as Edward the Seventh in 1901 the horse population of London was beginning to rear and plunge less painfully when these strange, large-wheeled, high-bodied, queer-smelling, and oddly-sounding objects invaded their domain.

From the end of the eighteenth century onwards compassionate men and women had been striving hard to lessen the vast burden of human and animal suffering, but the last

The first underground railway, 1863

'*Whiskered gentlemen waving their top-hats in the unroofed trucks that made the trial trip*'

From a contemporary engraving

bull-ring did not disappear from London till 1835, and though Lord Shaftesbury's Bill prohibiting the use of 'climbing boys' to sweep chimneys became law in 1840, it was twenty years or more before these pitiful little figures vanished from the streets. With them went an ancient and pleasing custom—the chimney-sweeps' May Day revel, when they danced to the sound of the fiddle, beating their dustpans

Little Chimney-Sweeps eating Penny Ices

Though Lord Shaftesbury's Bill abolishing the 'climbing boys' became law in 1840, these 'young Africans of our own growth' (as Charles Lamb called them) had not finally vanished from the streets of London fourteen years later

From 'Punch', 1854

with their brooms, and circling round one of their members who, decorated with leafy boughs, represented the traditional figure of Jack-in-the-Green— a pre-historic divinity honoured in the Thames valley long before the Romans came. What was needed—and what happened during the middle years of

Queen Victoria—was a general awakening of the public conscience. When that came, a great statesman[1] could boldly declare that 'the rights of labour are as sacred as the rights of property' without causing the Lord Mayor, Aldermen and Common Council to throw up their hands in horror.

'Penny-farthing' Bicycles and a ladies' Tricycle 'built for two' in the Park when the later Victorian age was at its peak

From 'Punch', 1883

As time passed the City dropped its age-long habit of meddling in politics, and gained proportionately in dignity and public esteem. But it did not drop—and has not dropped—its ancient customs and ceremonies. On state occasions the Lord Mayor goes forth as of yore in his gilded Cinderella coach, with two cock-hatted, gold-braided, silk-stockinged footmen hanging on behind and a coachman in a cauliflower wig perched proudly aloft on the box; he wears

[1] Benjamin Disraeli, Earl of Beaconsfield.

the chain presented by a former Lord Mayor in 1525; he still at the great banquets in the Guildhall receives his guests to the sound of fanfares, and feasts them on turtle-soup, while the City swords, hanging on the wall behind his chair, bear witness to the pride, the splendour, and the free spirit of London.

By the time that Queen Victoria died she had become an almost legendary figure, not so much the mother as the great-grandmother of her 'dear people', as she called them in her private diary. She was herself the last of the great Victorians and a fine example. But her memorial outside Buckingham Palace is completely Edwardian, with its winged image of Victory looking like an outsize fairy from some marble Christmas tree, and its large symbolical ladies each leading a handsome lion.

The reign of her son, Edward the Seventh, was comparatively brief—1901–10; but it marked the peak of Great Britain's worldly prosperity and power. It was a grandiose, flamboyant, too-heavily-ornamented age. Did we not hold, as Rudyard Kipling reminded us, 'dominion over palm and pine'? Was London not the centre of the greatest Empire in world history? Other Empires based on cruelty and oppression had crumbled away; but why should that fate overtake an Imperial Commonwealth founded on the loyalty of the various free peoples composing it?

Why should London worry if storm clouds darkened over the Balkan Peninsula, or if Germany started building a larger fleet than she could possibly need to patrol and defend her very limited coast-line? The Balkans were far away: and we could—and did—increase our Navy to keep pace with German naval expansion. Not since William the Norman burned Southwark in 1066 had the City seen the actual face of war.

The London streets hummed merrily as the twentieth

century moved on its way. Motor-cars of ever-increasing
speed and beauty multiplied; motor-buses, white ones driven
by steam and then red ones driven by petrol, enabled even

A 'Masher' hails a Hansom cab

*Twenty years later he would have been called a 'knut' and would have
hailed a taxi*

From 'Punch', 1894

the poorest people to take their families on frequent little
trips to the countryside instead of going only once or twice
a year by donkey cart to Hampstead Heath or by steamer to
Greenwich. Sir John Lubbock had instituted Bank Holidays

in 1871, but it was not until the first and second decades of the new century that the working population of London could enjoy them to the full.

Vanished are now the smiling Italian women turning the handle of a barrel-organ, the swarthy concertina-player with his morose, petticoated monkey, the muffin-man with his cheerful bell, the Punch and Judy show; vanished are the German bandsmen with their dingy wind instruments and their heavy spectacled faces. But from well-burnished instruments the red-and-blue clad members of the Salvation Army still produce heart-stirring tunes as they have done ever since 1878, when their founder, 'General' William Booth, created that remarkable body to aid him in his efforts to evangelize *Darkest England*.[1] The 'Pearly King' in his coat sewn all over with buttons, and his Queen, with her hat covered with feathers, are still to be seen at least once a year when a Harvest Festival service is held at their very own church, St. Mary Magdalene, Southwark.

In May, 1910, nine reigning sovereigns followed the coffin of Edward the Seventh through the London streets. No one then dreamed that eight years later a British Prime Minister[2] speaking at the Lord Mayor's banquet would declare with truth that 'empires and kingdoms and kings and crowns were falling like withered leaves before a gale'. Most of the royal mourners were resplendent in military uniforms but the new King, George the Fifth, was wearing the blue and gold of an Admiral of the Fleet. He was a sailor king, and he bore with the coolness, tenacity and courage of a sailor a burden such as no British monarch had ever yet been called upon to bear.

World War I was a small-scale rehearsal for World War II. The only ordeal which London escaped was the sight of victorious enemy troops marching through the City. She

---

[1] The title of his own book. [2] David Lloyd George on November 9, 1918.

was spared this again in World War II, but after the fall of the Channel ports in the summer of 1940 she was spared little else. Once more she had wise and indomitable leaders

'*His Usual Seat*'
An indomitable old Londoner during the Blitz
From '*Punch*', 1941

to beckon her along the steep and hard road to victory; once more her stout-hearted people were cheered by the example of a sailor King, George the Sixth of blessed memory, who was as stout-hearted as themselves.

The close of 1940 and the first months of 1941 were made terrible by the second Great Fire of London. Mr. Pepys[1] would have recognized the 'malicious, bloody flame' in the night sky, a pulsing orange glow visible from high ground many miles away. The river was for a time so choked with débris near the estuary that the tide could scarcely ebb or flow; the water turned black, the swans departed, no sea-gulls were seen or heard. Only one thing was unchanged— the valiant heart of London, which even the later menace of the manless missiles nicknamed the 'doodle-bugs' could not quell.

Future chroniclers will have many things to tell concerning those years, but this is not the place to linger over things so recent. This story may end where World War II ended, and a new, unwritten chapter of history began. Of the innumerable scenes which have been recorded, one above all the others seems worthy of perpetual remembrance. Great, rolling clouds of dark smoke hang over the burning City, touched here and there by reflected flame. And there, above the smoke and against the flame, two symbols rise, as they still rise today, symbols of human justice and divine mercy—the sworded figure on the dome of the Old Bailey and the golden cross on the dome of St. Paul's.

[1] See Chapter IX for the first Great Fire.